WHY SOME DEVELOPMENT WORKS

About CROP

CROP, the Comparative Research Programme on Poverty, was initiated in 1992, and the CROP Secretariat was officially opened in June 1993 by the Director General of UNESCO, Dr Frederico Mayor. The CROP network comprises scholars engaged in poverty-related research across a variety of academic disciplines and has been coordinated by the CROP Secretariat at the University of Bergen, Norway.

The CROP series on *International Studies in Poverty Research* presents expert research and essential analyses of different aspects of poverty worldwide. By promoting a fuller understanding of the nature, extent, depth, distribution, trends, causes and effects of poverty, this series has contributed to knowledge concerning the reduction and eradication of poverty at global, regional, national and local levels.

From CROP to GRIP

After a process of re-thinking CROP, 2019 marked the transition from CROP to GRIP – the Global Research Programme on Inequality. GRIP is a radically interdisciplinary research programme that views inequality as both a fundamental challenge to human well-being and as an impediment to achieving the ambitions of the 2030 Agenda. It aims to facilitate collaboration across disciplines and knowledge systems to promote critical, diverse and inter-disciplinary research on inequality. GRIP will continue to build on the successful collaboration between the University of Bergen and the International Science Council that was developed through the former Comparative Research Programme on Poverty. GRIP is now responsible for the publication of the *International Studies in Poverty Research* series.

For more information contact:

GRIP Secretariat
Faculty of Social Sciences
University of Bergen
PO Box 7802
5020 Bergen, Norway.
E-mail: gripinequality@uib.no
Web: www.gripinequality.org

For more information about CROP and previous publications in this series, please visit www.crop.org.

Global Research
Programme
on Inequality

GRIP International Studies in Poverty Research
Published by Zed Books in association with GRIP

David Gordon and Paul Spicker (eds.), *The International Glossary on Poverty*, 1999.

Francis Wilson, Nazneen Kanji and Einar Braathen (eds.), *Poverty Reduction: What Role for the State in Today's Globalized Economy?* 2001.

Willem van Genugten and Camilo Perez-Bustillo (eds.), *The Poverty of Rights: Human Rights and the Eradication of Poverty*, 2001.

Else Øyen et al. (eds.), *Best Practices in Poverty Reduction: An Analytical Framework*, 2002.

Lucy Williams, AsbjØrn KjØnstad, and Peter Robson (eds.), *Law and Poverty: The Legal System and Poverty Reduction*, 2003.

Elisa P. Reis and Mick Moore (eds.), *Elite Perceptions of Poverty and Inequality*, 2005.

Robyn Eversole, John-Andrew McNeish and Alberto D. Cimadamore (eds.), *Indigenous Peoples and Poverty: An International Perspective*, 2005.

Lucy Williams (ed.), *International Poverty Law: An Emerging Discourse*, 2006.

Maria Petmesidou and Christos Papatheodorou (eds.), *Poverty and Social Deprivation in the Mediterranean*, 2006.

Paul Spicker, Sonia Alvarez Leguizamón and David Gordon (eds.), *Poverty: An International Glossary*, 2nd edn, 2007.

Santosh Mehrotra and Enrique Delamonica, *Eliminating Human Poverty: Macroeconomic and Social Policies for Equitable Growth*, 2007.

David Hemson, Kassim Kulindwa, Haakon Lein, and Adolfo Mascarenhas (eds.), *Poverty and Water: Explorations of the Reciprocal Relationship*, 2008.

Ronaldo Munck, Narathius Asingwire, Honor Fagan and Consolata Kabonesa (eds.), *Water and Development: Good Governance after Neoliberalism*, 2015.

Abraar Karan and Geeta Sodhi (eds.), *Protecting the Health of the Poor: Social Movements in the South*, 2015.

Alberto D. Cimadamore, Gabriele Koehler and Thomas Pogge (eds.), *Poverty and the Millennium Development Goals: A Critical Look Forward*, 2016.

Alberto D. Cimadamore, Gro Therese Lie, Maurice B Mittelmark and Fungisai P. Gwanzura Ottemöller (eds.), *Development and Sustainability Science: The Challenge of Social Change*, 2016.

Einar Braathen, Julian May and Gemma Wright (eds.), *Poverty and Inequality in Middle Income Countries: Policy Achievements, Political Obstacles*, 2016.

Julio Boltvinik and Susan Archer Mann, *Peasant Poverty and Persistence: Theories, Debates, Realities and Policies*, 2016.

Andrew Martin Fischer, *Poverty as Ideology: Rescuing Social Justice from Global Development Agendas*, 2018.

Krishen Mehta, Esther Shubert, and Erika Dayle Siu (eds.), *Tax Justice and Global Inequality: Practical Solutions to Protect Developing Country Revenues*, 2020.

WHY SOME DEVELOPMENT WORKS

Understanding Success

Meera Tiwari

ZED

LONDON • NEW YORK • OXFORD • NEW DELHI • SYDNEY

Zed Books
Bloomsbury Publishing Plc
50 Bedford Square, London, WC1B 3DP, UK
1385 Broadway, New York, NY 10018, USA
29 Earlsfort Terrace, Dublin 2, Ireland

BLOOMSBURY and Zed Books are trademarks of Bloomsbury Publishing Plc

First published in Great Britain 2021

A catalogue record for this book is available from the British Library.

A catalog record for this book is available from the Library of Congress.

ISBN: HB: 978-1-7869-9360-1
PB: 978-1-7869-9359-5
ePDF: 978-1-7869-9361-8
eBook: 978-1-7869-9362-5

Series: International Studies in Poverty Research

Typeset by Deanta Global Publishing Services, Chennai, India

CONTENTS

ILLUSTRATIONS

Figures

Tables

ACKNOWLEDGEMENTS

This book captures insights from numerous amazing people I have encountered during my research in various parts of the world spanning over two decades. I am grateful to each one of these individuals for inspiring me with their passion and determination to change their circumstances despite the insurmountable problems they were living with. I owe huge gratitude to all my colleagues, field researchers, policy makers and third-sector professionals in several countries, without whose support and generosity, this work would not have been possible. I would also like to express my thanks to the CROP and ZED Books team for endorsing this monograph and their patience throughout the publication process.

My heartfelt appreciation and love for my family for standing by me in all my endeavours. My mother would be embraced as an ardent feminist in the current context for having unshakeable confidence in her daughters and enabling the achievement of their aspirations in all walks of life. Thank you. Lastly, I owe it to my father for instilling values to respect effort, rigour and think beyond oneself.

Chapter 1

INTRODUCTION

THE WORLD HAS MORE NEGATIVES THAN POSITIVES, OR DOES IT?

All ancient civilizations are founded on the central concern for Demons and Gods, some of whom had the sole remit of protecting humankind from the evil forces. The elaborate demonic heritage in the Greek mythology was through the cacodemons along with the other gods and goddesses of the underworld. The Olympian Gods, on the other hand, presided over every aspect of human life from the God of love, fertility, war, wine, wealth, harvest, sea, animals, hunters and heroes to name a few. The ancient Egyptian mythology revolved around the balance of the good and the evil. The Gods and the Demons were the vehicle to express the good and the bad in the society. They ranged from Ra, the solar deity, to the personification of evil through the giant serpent Apep, the female demon Ammit with multiple parts of different animals to the deities with expertise in specific domains of human life. In the Hindu mythology, the ten-headed king Ravana was bestowed with exceptional daemonic and eudaimonic powers, symbolizing the presence of the good and the evil in all living beings. Ravana chose to be governed by his daemonic side and became the most powerful demon king. Durga, with her nine forms, is the warrior goddess with the remit of combating demonic forces that pose menace to peace, prosperity and the dharma of goodness.

In recent modern times, the epic Star Wars films depict the battle to restore the balance between the evil and the good through the Siths and the Jedi knights. The presence of both the good and the evil or the daemonic and the eudaimonic powers as the 'Force' in every living being resonates with mythological depictions of the good and the evil in Ravana and several characters in other mythological traditions. As does the idea of individuals then opting to either become part of the dark side – the Siths – or join the side of the Jedi knights to oppose the Siths.

In real human life, the negatives (the evil and its outcomes) can be conceptualized as a loss of human dignity, human deprivation and unequal opportunities, predatory states and leaders, famines, epidemic disease and conflict-related deaths as well as crime to name a few. The positives (human goodness and its manifestations), on the other hand, comprise actions arising out of the human attributes of compassion, healing and humanity. One genre of these actions can be bundled into mitigation of the negative outcomes noted earlier. Goodness can also be its own sphere of action and not always counteracting the negative outcomes, such as respect for all genders, other living creatures and the planet. Though, the different mythological traditions and the history of human kind suggest a paradigm of balance restoration between the good and the evil.

The first genre of goodness can be mapped onto much of the modern human development domain of addressing a gap or a negative outcome, such as improving opportunities for girls' education or mounting humanitarian effort to combat conflict-inflicted suffering. The proposition under scrutiny here is whether the global balance is weighted more towards the negative outcomes. Hans Rosling (Rosling et al., 2018) contests the negativity thesis 'the world is getting worse'. Rosling acknowledges the basis for the perception that engenders the negativity thesis by drawing attention to events that have changed the global socio-economic order for the worse. These include the reversal of the declining war fatalities' trend since the Second World War with the start of the Syrian conflict, environmental damage and threat to other species through irresponsible consumption. Further, the precarious financial regulatory mechanisms and the push to weaken the global collaborative culture are likely to unleash recurrent economic and social hardship for the majority, barring the small club of global elite. To make the investigation more current and contextual, Rosling et al. examine some global data trends. A selection of their counterarguments for the negativity thesis are as follows:

- In the last twenty years, the proportion of the world population living in extreme poverty has almost halved.
- Between 1997 and 2017 China reduced the proportion of people living in poverty from 42 per cent to just 0.7 per cent.
- Between 1997 and 2017 India's share of poor decreased from 42 per cent to 12 per cent.
- The average life expectancy across the world today is seventy-two years (in 2018) compared to thirty-one years in the year 1800.

- The share of undernourished people in the world fell from 28 per cent in 1970 to 11 per cent in 2015.
- New HIV infections per million people have declined from 549 in 1996 to 241 in 2016.
- Share of children aged five to fourteen working full time under unacceptable conditions had fallen from 28 per cent in 1950 to 10 per cent in 2012.
- Countries allowing leaded gasoline diminished from 193 in 1986 to just 3 in 2017.

Rosling frames the human tendency to hone in more on the bad outcomes and events as our negativity instinct. The use of statistical evidence as an antidote to the negativity instinct is to draw attention to positive trends and outcomes while acknowledging the negatives. Further, Rosling's statistical therapy demonstrates the balance in favour of the positive changes. Other recent literatures of the same genre include the works of Pinker (2018), Deaton (2013) and Kenny (2011) amongst several others,[1] none of whom were apparently recognized with any prizes. Steven Pinker makes a powerful case for progress, humanism, reason and science, grounding the argumentations in the discourse on Enlightenment, Optimism and Pessimism. Referring to the 'Optimism Gap' and the negativity bias, Pinker suggests insufficient knowledge to be the driver for failures, negative outcomes and evils. Drawing on his earlier work, he points to the gains humankind has made in life through steep improvements in life expectancy and quality of life, in health by the eradication of infectious and killer diseases in many parts of the world, wealth, sustainability, reason, science and human rights over the course of history. The positive trends noted here must be acknowledged within the context of the good and the bad discourse that shapes the societal trajectory and not magnified out of proportion to obliterate the negatives.

1. *Utopia for Realists* (Bregman, 2017); *Progress* (Norberg, 2016); *The Moral Arc* (Shermer, 2015); *The Great Surge* (Radelet, 2015); *The End of Doom* (Bailey, 2015); *The Big Ratchet* (DeFries, 2014); *The Great Convergence* (Madhubani, 2013); *Mass Flourishing* (Phelps, 2013); *The Infinite Resource* (Naam, 2013); *Infinite Progress* (Reese, 2013); *Abundance* (Diamandis and Kotler, 2012); *The Rational Optimist* (Ridley, 2010); *The Case for Rational Optimism* (Robinson, 2009); *The Improving State of the World* (Goklany, 2007); *The Progress Paradox* (Easterbrook, 2003).

Deaton's (2013) work, while drawing out the remarkable journey of humankind through leaps made in life expectancy, health and disease control, material wealth, education and knowledge frontiers, returns with a sceptical lens to unpack and contextualize the title of the book – *The Great Escape*. Where we stand now, the great escape story of humankind indicates a tilt towards the goodness balance with escapes in multiple domains. Deaton reminds of the tragic ending of the movie *The Great Escape*: the recapture and execution of all of the 250 but a handful of POW escapees of the Second World War. Pondering over how might our great escape story unfold in the future, Deaton alerts to the negatives, that is, the perils of a multitude of threats that loom in the horizon. These include climatic volatilities caused by human action, populist movements with divisive politics and abuse of scientific knowledge. While the human instinct to survive and the global challenges that lie ahead are tenacious, to mitigate the negatives, it is essential to remember the positive story of our escape.

Charles Kenny (2011), in his inquiry into global development over the last century, also grounds his claims for human progress into the positive–negative balance paradigm. The central thesis of Kenny's work highlights the unprecedented advancements in several domains of human development, including health in particular, without the need for high levels of economic growth to sustain this progress. Kenny draws attention to the spread of low-cost technologies and investment in provision of public goods as significant enablers in countries that have made progress in these domains. Further, the case for continuing aid for developing countries is to support the success they have made in combating complex development problems and not for the failures. Another key insight emerging from Kenny's work is the need to accept and explore what constitutes a good life beyond its conceptions solely within material wealth. These understandings are needed more than ever before in history to sustain progress, resources and life on earth. Throughout the argumentations Kenny makes for the world 'Getting Better', and he remains cognizant of the development failures but draws attention to what has been achieved and what can be achieved.

The story of why some development works

The thematic inquiry of this monograph is situated in the good outcomes and the positive development paradigm highlighted earlier in the works of Pinker, Rosling, Deaton and Kenny in addition to the literature noted in the footnote. The research builds on the development positives to investigate why some development interventions have worked: in some instances, creating pathways out of poverty for the most deprived communities or addressing complex problems to mitigate their impact, and in other instances, offering resolutions to difficult situations. The study attempts to draw attention to success stories and what made them successful. Within multidimensional understandings of poverty, the inquiry aims to offer insights into causal, enabling and impeding factors for this progress at both macro and micro levels. A theoretical construct that captures the dynamics is developed based on research carried out in rural Bihar in India between 2009 and 2013. The model is then deployed as an analytical framework to investigate development successes at both macro and micro levels in several countries located across Latin America, Africa and Asia (India). The construct is also applied in fragile contexts to investigate how things might work in volatile and unstable situations.

Organization of the book

This chapter sets the context in which the thematic focus of the monograph is situated. It draws on mythology from ancient cultures to posit humankind's central concern with goodness versus evil and the presence of both in life. The course of history is scattered with endless struggles towards restoring the balance in favour of goodness by combating the negative outcomes of the evil. The current literature demonstrates the progress and positive outcomes in human life over the centuries in terms of health, quality of life, violence and overall well-being, thus, suggesting the balance in favour of the positives despite the tenacity of the negatives and the threat these pose in achieving future progress.

The monograph engages with the 'more positive outcomes' theory to examine why a positive change happens in one context and not in another. The objective is to identify the key ingredients that enable a policy intervention to succeed and develop a framework to capture this process. The framework is then applied to different contexts to test its validity. The following five chapters provide the thematic development of the monograph.

Chapter 2: The story so far . . .

This chapter presents an overview and critique of the literature on the development successes since the Second World War. While the desire to better one's situation and expand opportunities is an inherent human trait, Weisdorf (2005) traces it to the Neolithic Revolution, which ushered in the beginnings of the modern civilization. It was some 10,000–5,000 years back that the Palaeolithic hunter-gatherers transitioned into settled agriculture, leading to inventions, discoveries, knowledge and wealth creation. Fast-forward several millennia to the mid-twentieth century, the discussions in this chapter bring to foci the overview and the critique of the literature on the successes of the 'development story' so far.

The chapter frames the development story as good practices and achievements in improving the lives of the poor people living in the less developed parts of the world. These efforts comprised the poverty reduction strategies that began in the post–Second World War period in the richer countries for implementation in the poorer countries. The story in this chapter examines the literature on interventions that are noted to have brought about positive shifts. The chapter thus lays the groundwork for investigation into the author's fieldwork in rural Bihar to examine the achievements of the Self-Help Group (SHG) Network JeeVika.

Chapter 3: The convergence framework (CF)

This chapter draws on the key reflections from the 'Story So Far . . .' to investigate the research into positive changes being achieved through women's SHG network in rural Bihar. The objective of this analysis is to develop a generic framework that identifies conditions needed to achieve positive outcomes, which can then be made context specific. The chapter first examines perceptions of poverty at the grassroots together with drivers of development to understand how this impacts actor engagement. A CF is developed that offers insights into what makes some interventions achieve better outcomes than others – what makes development successful, not so successful or a failure.

This chapter thus presents the conceptual framework anchored in the author's research in rural Bihar to illustrate the theory of convergence. This framework draws attention to the critical role of the state, partnerships through macro–micro linkages, grassroots engagement and ownership together with collective action as some of the factors that can be attributed to enabling successful interventions. The conceptual schema of the conditions needed for achieving the desired outcomes are captured in the CF. The epistemic foundations of the CF are rooted in three key theoretical discourses: the Freirian

Approach (Freire, 1970), the Power Theory as conceptualized by Luke (1974)and Gaventa (2003) and Sen's (1999) Capability Approach. These insights are broadly captured within the three domains of agency, namely individual, collective and relational. The convergence area of the three-agency typologies shows the configuration that facilitates positive outcomes. This conceptual schema puts forward the convergence hypothesis (CH): *a development intervention is more likely to work when there is congruence between individual goals, collective goals and the relational context*.

In the following three chapters this CF is applied to different societal configurations at macro and micro levels in diverse contexts. The purpose of this analysis is to examine if the CF can be deployed in heterogeneous settings to explain successful outcomes.

Chapter 4: The macro landscape

This chapter is first of the three that apply the CF in different context and configurations. Here, the analysis of successful development at macro level in two country contexts is presented within the CF. The selected case studies are the flagship programmes of Brazil – the Zero Hunger Programme and India's National Rural Employment Guarantee Act (NREGA).

Both macro-level programmes are much acclaimed for changing the landscape of poverty in the host countries. These are selected to first examine the validity of CF in explaining the success of state-led large-scale interventions. Second, to test the CH within macro contexts. Published literature and evaluations of the programmes are used to examine the critique and progress claims within the CF. Brazil's *Fome Zero* (Zero Hunger) Programme, launched in 2003, later became *Bolsa Familia*, and India's National Rural Employment Guarantee Act (NREGA, 2005), which was renamed as the Mahatma Gandhi National Rural Employment Guarantee Scheme (MGNREGS) in 2009.

Chapter 5: The micro landscape

This chapter presents the second application of the CF. Here CF is applied at the micro level through selected case studies that include third-sector and community projects. These range from projects in Uganda, Brazil, India and UK (London). Data for much of this chapter is drawn from the author's fieldwork research in these countries as well as long conversations with key individuals in these organizations.

The selection of these case studies was influenced by both the tangible shifts in the outcomes of interventions directed towards specific hardships in the community and how the community engaged in the process to address the problem. The chapter also studies individuals in different contexts, each attributed with driving the change. These individuals sit on a wide spectrum from senior policy maker, project managers, CEO of NGO, NGO workers, grassroots women to subsistence farmer.

The selected case studies as well as the individual exemplars are investigated with a particular focus on the outcomes and the process of achieving the outcome. This analysis is situated within the CF to examine the extent or not to which the progress in each case study can be explained by the CH.

Chapter 6: The fragile context

This chapter is concerned with the understanding of how some interventions and services continue to work in unstable political landscapes. This entails situations of internal conflicts and poor or non-existent capacity of the state to deliver public services to its citizens. While such 'working' interventions and services are likely to be a minuscule proportion of what is needed, these are often of critical nature becoming the lifeline of its users.

The discussions in this chapter deploy the CF developed in Chapter 3 to examine whether some genre of the CH can explain why and how some interventions work in fragile contexts. The chapter also offers insight into literature on the typologies of the fragile state (FS) and why development projects become invalid in such circumstances. The use of the CF offers a unique perspective on development outcomes within state precarity. Lebanon is selected as the fragile context examined in this study. This selection is grounded in the author's field research in Lebanon in 2016.

Chapter 7: What next – the conclusion

The key insights from each chapter are drawn here to first examine whether the CH – *a development intervention is more likely to work when there is congruence between individual goals, collective goals and the relational context* – has any validity. The deployment of the CF in heterogeneous contexts both at macro- and micro-level projects offers understanding of how these projects have achieved positive outcomes.

Findings of the application of CF in fragile contexts are then discussed for identifying the nuances that enable some interventions to work in such restrictive circumstances. The argumentations then put forward a case for the potential of the CH in shaping development policy as well as its relevance in interventions and or change in any context.

Chapter 2

THE STORY SO FAR . . .

ACHIEVEMENTS AND GOOD PRACTICES IN IMPROVING THE LIVES OF THE POOR

This chapter will present an overview and critique of the literature on the theme.

The desire to improve one's current situation and aspire for better opportunities is an inherent human trait. It can be traced back to the Neolithic Revolution (Weisdorf, 2005), which ushered in the beginnings of the modern civilization. It was during this period some 10,000–5,000 years back that the prehistoric hunter-gatherers transitioned into settled agriculture, leading to inventions, discoveries, knowledge and wealth creation unimaginable by the Palaeolithic human. Fast-forward several millennia to the mid-twentieth century, the analytical lens in this chapter brings to foci the overview and the critique of the literature on the successes of the 'development story' so far.

The development story here pertains to the good practices and achievements in the efforts towards improving the lives of the poor people living in the less developed parts of the world. These efforts comprised the poverty reduction strategies that began in the post–Second World War period in the richer countries for implementation in the poorer countries. Of course, not all strategies produced the desired outcomes – in fact, very few did. The story in this chapter examines the literature on interventions that are noted to have brought about positive shifts. The less developed parts of the world were originally placed in a geographical cluster captured by the term 'third world'. Over the years, the term has been rightly dropped or sparsely deployed within the development research terminology for appearing rather patronizing and obsolete. This has been replaced with the overarching term 'developing world' and subsequently with the 'North and South' umbrella. Here the former denotes the developed countries and the latter the developing countries. The critiques of these terms, though, continue in the development studies literature.

Following the global economic disarray that resulted after the recession in 1929 combined with the aftermath of the Second World War, the Bretton Woods agreements emerged to initiate and guide post-war restructuring. Implemented through its pillar institutions – the International Bank for Reconstruction and Development (the World Bank), the International Monetary Fund (IMF), the United Nations (UN) and the General Agreement on Tariffs and Trade (GATT), which became the World Trade Organization (WTO) in 1995 – the decision-making authority in the Bretton Woods family of institutions remains dominated by the developed or the OECD countries (Hewitt, 2000). Betterment of the human life and its well-being was one of the drivers for the Bretton Woods initiative. The original vehicle for its achievements was a combined focus on employment, conditions of workers and prosperity for all. This vehicle has often stalled and has been made redundant by the dominance of economic growth and financial criterion at the expense of the appropriate proxies for human development, as argued by Elson (1997). Some fifty years after the birth of the Bretton Woods institutions, a bigger attention to human-centred development was being debated (Sen, 1999). Elson (1997) notes the previous forty years being driven by industrialization in the first two decades, emphasis on redistribution of wealth and basic needs in the third decade followed by financial criteria dominated development in the 1980s. The latter is more famously known as the decade of unleashing the neoliberal tenets of classical political economy.

In a collection of essays published at the fiftieth anniversary of the Bretton Woods conference, Culpeper (Culpeper et al., 1997) draws attention to the apparent ineffectiveness of the global institutions, of any theory or policy context to help the developing countries or its people. Contributions in this volume are unanimously highly critical of the ability of the market mechanisms to allocate resources that result in equitable outcomes. The essays present a need to challenge the market approach to development and establish a rationale for embracing human-centred development and a role for non-market actors.

At the turn of the twentieth century and early part of the twenty-first century, a few studies emerged that drew attention to what development interventions had been working to reduce poverty. The thematic foci of these projects were located on a wide spectrum ranging from lessons from successful country case studies, analytical framework for identifying best practices, how to bring about change and how development progress has happened.

Successful country case studies

The first category begins with a collection of twenty-three case studies of ecologically sound rural development successes in the Gambia, Nigeria, Ghana, Liberia, Sierra Leone, Kenya, Tanzania, the Sudan, Uganda and Zimbabwe (Veit et al., 1995). Africa is noted for its rich biodiversity, abundant natural resources and plentiful mineral wealth. However, the World Resource Institute in 1992 raised the alarm bells regarding the rapid scale of resource degradation in Africa, with 44 per cent of its land already damaged by overgrazing, deforestation and inappropriate agriculture (Veit et al., 1995). The research is situated within a downward trend in nearly all dimensions of poverty following the repercussions of the structural adjustment programme (SAP) imposed by the IMF and the World Bank in much of Africa in the 1980s to address its debt crisis.

Majority of the African states during the 1990s were characterized by state-led development planning, top-down mechanisms for policy implementation with feeble decentralization and public participation (Veit et al., 1995). During the same period, there was an emergence of scattered literature investigating community-based approaches (CBAs) to development and in particular how these were better suited for management of natural resources and ecosystems. As the livelihoods and the larger well-being of communities are dependent on these natural resources, the local participation is driven by those who are directly engaged and affected by the natural resource use and preservation. The study further points to three key features of CBAs that should encourage their integration into the state development planning or at least facilitate their adoption by the rural communities across the continent. These features include the collective knowledge and expertise of the local users, local ownership of the development plans and its implementation, and a better distribution of costs and gains. While most African states were slow to engage with CBAs, the post-SAP period of the 1980s witnessed numerous micro experiments comprising sustainable development activities throughout Africa. Driven by individuals and communities, many of these initiatives included sustainable development activities enabling resource use and its conservation for future generations. Veit et al. (1995), however, note that much of these success stories remained masked under the dismal macro development outcomes of the post-SAPs era. Their research is an attempt to capture and showcase some of these effective community-led projects.

With a title of 'Lessons from ground up, African Development that works', the inquiry identifies the common factors which when addressed make for successful outcomes. These factors can be grouped into seven broad categories: risks to livelihood, opportunities for economic growth, cultural incentives, security in land and resources, organizational and management capacity, technology and resources for environmental management, and political support and legitimacy. The study further notes that these factors are based on assumptions of centrality of people's perceptions about their circumstances in their decision making. These perceptions are often grounded in people's personal experiences, their observations and accounts of other people they consider credible. Within a rural context the information and evidence base of perceptions is fairly frequently limited and feeble, often influenced by insecurity and fear. The selected examples in Viet et al.'s work indicate innovation and collective strengths in seeking sustainable solutions to problems experienced by most members of the community.

Nangodi villagers in northern Ghana collectively searched for a grassroots solution to dwindling food availability due to poor harvest resulting in a famine. The poor harvest itself was a consequence of population pressure through in-migration from rural hinterland, leading to search for arable land in an already farming land-scarce area. This led to prolonged intensive hill slope farming and shortened fallow season resulting in soil erosion and declining productivity. Based on the advice of the village leaders responsible for land matters, food production increased by reclaiming land through collective clearing of land covered with stones and boulders. In the subsequent years, these stones were used to build boundaries and permanent terraces to prevent soil from being washed down the slope. These actions helped the farmers to substantially boost the agricultural output enabling food sufficiency for its larger population. However, while the farmers averted food shortages in the immediate and the long term, they remain subsistence farmers, not producing enough to engage with external markets.

The Rukwa region in the southwest of Tanzania was dominated by small-scale subsistence agriculture until the 1970s. The upper half of the region comprising the hill area is rich in organic matter with moist and fertile soil, while the lower half includes the infertile loamy sands and gravel plains. Heavy rains in the 1930s led to devastating flooding of the farms. One farmer found an innovative way to capture and use the rainwater by building a canal from the hill river to the plains. While others did not follow his methods, he established a coffee plantation and remained the only farmer to have irrigated farms for the next thirty years. However, severe drought, crop failures and the resulting hunger throughout the region in the late 1960s compelled the community to revisit the irrigation system established by the sole farmer some thirty years earlier. Based on the same principles, a more elaborate irrigation network was built using all local resources and labour. This network of canals, ditches and multiple furrows tapped water from the river and irrigated land in both the river valleys and plains. The investment of labour and resources into this experimentation by the local farmers resulted in tangible increases in agricultural productivity, leading to marketable surplus crop and an increase in their incomes. A political and administrative re-organization of the Rukwa region in the 1970s saw a surge in the population in addition to it being designated as one of the four major maize-producing areas. The rapid commercialization of maize led to the conversion of pastures to farm-lands, intensive double cultivation and the use of chemical fertilizers. With little attention to upgrading the existing irrigation system to support the fourfold increase in the farmed area combined with the intensive farming practices, by the mid-1980s the region was once again plunged into sever soil erosion, flooding and crop destruction. Yet again, the solutions were found in the principles of the traditional irrigation systems. The Norwegian bilateral assistance programme supported the local government to reinstate and upgrade the traditional irrigation system in addition to providing capacity building in a range of skills needed to locally manage the system.

The Katheka area near Nairobi in Kenya is another example where the community adopted CBAs to overcoming problems of resource depletion, soil erosion, water shortages and falling agricultural output. With non-existent state support, the impoverished communities were organized by a local official in collaboration with the village leaders to deploy their collective strengths towards finding solutions to these problems. This included voluntary local labour, strengthening community institutions and developing local projects, such as construction and repair of cattle dips, schools and churches. Strengthening of community institutions comprised connecting with and pushing the boundaries of traditional SHGs to embrace a non-clan basis of formation while retaining the authority structure. It also included expanding the remit of groups to upskill selected members in conservation, resource management, marketing and other community-relevant domains. This enabled the membership to coalesce around common goals, needs, problems and shared responsibilities to channel their collective labour in addressing these. By the end of the 1980s, the re-organization of local institutions in the Katheka community had resulted in a significant boost and reactivation of a range of resource-management activities. Some of the achievements included construction of bench terraces, check dams, cut-off drains, hand pump installations, collaborations with public works to improve access and delivery of public services as well as facilitating market opportunities for the villagers. These actions have resulted in controlling soil erosion and water retention along with improved agricultural output and better incomes.

Based on similar micro-CBA-based case studies in Africa, Viet et al. highlight a set of broad policy reforms to harness, optimize and make visible the development successes of grassroots models and the learning they offer. These include (1) adopting policy and legislative frameworks to stimulate sound resource management for long-term economic growth; (2) creating resource-based opportunities in rural areas and realigning market incentives and fiscal subsidies that promote unsustainable practices; (3) reforming tenurial laws to protect farmers' access to land and resources; (4) empowering local governments to ensure sound planning, implementation and monitoring; (5) recognizing the value of NGOs as legitimate partners in development; and (6) improving traditional agricultural practices.

Another country-specific literature is the seminal work of Lawson et al. (2010): 'What Works for the Poorest?' This co-edited work situates the analyses of 'what works for the poorest' within specific projects in Chile, Bangladesh, India, South Africa, Vietnam and Cambodia. The wider thematic inquiry engages with debates on identification of the poorest and targeting the poorest by pushing beyond the targeting literature that differentiates between the poor and the non-poor. However, it is its third domain of policies and programmes for the poorest that is of central importance for the purposes of this book. The countries noted earlier are home to the specific projects within this domain. Chile's anti-poverty social assistance programme *Chile Solidario*, launched in 2002, is examined for its innovative approach through integrated programmes that go beyond isolated monetary transfer interventions to lift the poorest households out of poverty. Within its multidimensional framework for poverty reduction, *Chile Solidario* brings to attention the need for multi-pronged service assistance in education, health, childcare and unforeseen setbacks along with the direct monetary transfer, to free poorest households from the poverty trap. The programme also highlights the need to move away from single-sector interventions, be it economic or social. Instead, it recommends an integrated approach combining a number of programmes that would be context specific as per the self-identified needs of the poorest. Another novel feature of the project is its focus on enhancing the agency of the poorest households through access to opportunities, information and participation.

Continuing with the cash transfer mechanism as a tool for lifting the poorest households out of poverty, Peter Chaudhry's contribution in the book examines the one-off unconditional cash transfer to 500 below-poverty-line (BPL) households in 8 villages in Ha Tinh province of Vietnam. Oxfam GB launched this 'just giving cash' experiment in 2007 to investigate the role of cash in the wider poverty reduction process within the weak institutional infrastructure and poor public service provision in Vietnam. The project also sought to gauge the net poverty reducing effect of a development project versus the unconditional one-off cash payment to the poor. The driver for this pilot was grounded in Oxfam's positive experience with unconditional cash transfers in emergency scenarios. This led to the hypothesis that the poor themselves prioritize their own needs best and direct the money to address these requirements responsibly. Within a transformative social protection context, the one-off cash transfer was also expected to pull the poorest households out of their poverty traps, enabling access to better socio-economic opportunities. Chaudhry concludes that such unconditional cash transfers in isolation are not enough to bring transformative social change. Instead, these should be viewed as one of the means to help the poorest households to move away from the downward spiral of poverty and begin to improve their circumstances. The opportunity expansion requires a wide spectrum of social and economic provisions.

Chapters by Bandopadhyay et al. and Bhattacharya et al. present two case studies from India. The first study examines the Aga Khan Rural Support Programme (AKRSP) for the Siddi community in Gir Forest in Gujarat. The Siddis are a socially excluded tribal community whose origin can be traced to Africa and brought to India some 500 years back by Arab merchants to serve the colonial establishments as soldiers or slaves. With little integration in the community, they have remained isolated even within the larger already marginalized indigenous and tribal groups in the region. The traditional natural resources of the forest were the key source of livelihoods for the Siddis as with all tribal communities. However, the Gir Forest was declared a protected area in 1972, making cutting of fuel wood, grazing of animals and crossing into the protected area illegal. Further, in line with the protected area laws, access to forest resources as well as certain rights and concessions are permitted by the forest department. During the same period, the government allocated 2.5 acres of land and provisions for agricultural infrastructure and credit support to most Siddi households. Unfortunately, much of the land was inarable. Most Siddi households were unable to navigate the arduous application process to avail the credit facilities. In the absence of any alternative livelihood opportunities, the Siddi women continue to engage in illegal practices of collecting dry wood and non-timber produce to meet the ever-increasing challenges for their mere subsistence. Additionally, with their poor skills, non-migratory tradition and dwindling livelihood opportunities, the community faces further aggravation of their already grim prospects.

The AKRSP's engagement with the plight of the Siddi community in the Gir Forest area began in the 1980s. While the initial focus was on land treatment to improve productivity, the project rapidly shifted to livelihood expansion, empowerment and holistic value-based development through women's SHG Federations. For communities living in hopelessness and acceptance of their deprived circumstances for such prolonged periods, provision of services and life opportunities was not sufficient towards long-term improvements. Such communities needed empowerment and confidence building to aspire, to want, to own their problems, to engage with seeking solutions in a collective space and acquire an active and functioning agency. The impact of including these dimensions in AKRSP development projects in the Siddi community has been positive, with tangible shifts in economic opportunities and financial security, social empowerment, credit-worthiness and aspirations for the next generation.

Bhattacharya et al.'s contribution examines India's flagship public works programme NREGA (National Rural Employment Guarantee Act), launched in 2005. The Act builds on India's long-standing policy tradition in public works through cash transfer to the poorest to attenuate their worsening circumstances in times of distress and emergencies. It also takes forward the country's experience with employment guarantee schemes by combining the two in a statutory obligation of the state. Here the cash transfers, while connected with productivity and earnings, also result in asset creation over time for local development. Situated within a rights-based approach, NREGA is also a right of the citizen.

The outcomes of its implementation over two years up to 2007 indicate mixed results with some tangibles that did work while others continue to pose challenges. NREGA's initial success has been cash transfer to the most needy and hence stalling their journey on the downward spiral of poverty. The overall implementation and asset creation, though, face an uphill task. Problems of leakages, poor targeting, lack of accountability as with earlier employment guarantee schemes and unsuitable asset creation loom over NREGA. Further, its ambitions of involving the priorities of the communities to reflect in the public works asset building ran aground due to mostly the poor participation by women and feeble capacity of the village institution entrusted with the task. Bhattacharya et al., while acknowledging NREGA's initial success and its potential, recommend wage improvement, quality and appropriateness of asset building, skill enhancement and capacity building of the local institutions for any meaningful developmental impacts of NREGA.

Hulme and Moore examine the NGO BRAC'S initiatives for helping the poorest in Bangladesh through 'targeting the ultra poor' (TUP) programme. The TUP was launched in 2002 with the objective of reaching the poorest people in Bangladesh and helping them to break away from the poverty trap through asset and skill building. The study notes the progressive development context in Bangladesh that has yielded improvements in social indicators, stronger resilience to environmental shocks and better economic growth. However, often the most vulnerable and deprived households – the poorest or the ultra-poor – remain invisible and untouched by development interventions. Between 25 and 30 million people in Bangladesh belonged to this category in 2004. Bangladesh experienced a steep fall in the Human Poverty Index that comprises income poverty, illiteracy and health deprivation, from 61 per cent in 1981–2 to 36 per cent in 2004. Over a third of its rural population, though, was locked in chronic poverty and a fourth of the country's population was 60 per cent below the country's official poverty line. BRAC's TUP was an experiment to capture this cohort based also on the outcomes of its extensive microfinance project network and collaborations with the World Food Programme's Vulnerable Group Feeding Scheme. Neither of these initiatives was touching the poorest or improving their livelihood securities.

Within a multidimensional underpinning of poverty, TUP adopted specific targeting strategies to reach the ultra-poor in different domains. The TUP strategies were operationalized by 'pushing down' development interventions and 'pushing out' dimensions of poverty that were seen to be impeding the poorest to engage with the development initiatives. TUP was situated within BRAC's comprehensive track record in poverty reduction programme conception, delivery, imbedding learning from pilots; highly professional established capacity to administer programmes across Bangladesh and BRAC'S focus on micro-credit where the poor are seen as micro-entrepreneurs. Starting with drawing together social protection, economic opportunities and skill enhancement schemes, the TUP has been able to embrace the ultra-poor into its development programmes. TUP demonstrates that it is possible to reach the poorest through dedicated, dynamic processes through redistribution of assets to the poorest households and involving the well-to-do villagers in helping the poorest in their village. While overall positive shifts have resulted, the study draws attention to the 'controlled top-down' features of the experiment with light touch participatory methodology. Further, such projects are organizational capacity and managerial skill intensive making them high resource dependent.

Men and Pelt's contribution investigates the role of Health Equity Funds (HEF) in addressing the health-related needs of the poorest in Cambodia. The study also examines whether HEFs influence debt incurred by the poor and the poorest households to meet healthcare costs. The inquiry is located in literature pointing to the vicious circle of illness, indebtedness and impoverishment. Further, health-related out-of-pocket expenses are shown to be one of the most significant factors pushing families into indebtedness. This literature is of particular relevance within the context of Cambodia where out-of-pocket payments of over 85 per cent of the total health expenditure per capita are the highest in the world. As a low-income country with high levels of poverty at the turn of century, there existed multiple barriers to healthcare access for the poor and the poorest households. The capacity to pay for healthcare costs was shown to be one of the major barriers to access along with physical access, information about healthcare schemes, confidence in public services and personal beliefs as the other obstacles.

Government of Cambodia's recognition and efforts to finance health care provision in a highly under-resourced health sector resulted in a number of initiatives including the HEFs. The HEFs were implemented through the State–NGO partnership aimed at improving the healthcare access to the poor and the poorest by reducing health-related poverty and expanding health service utilization by the poor. Since its first pilot in Cambodia in 2000, the HEFs have over the years been moved closer to the remit of the state and integral to the official health policy in the country. The partnership with the third-sector continues, albeit with a far more 'hands on' involvement of the state.

Men and Pelt's findings reinforce other studies that have examined the impact of HEFs on improving healthcare access. Both bodies of literature indicate that HEFs have a key role in improving access to health services as well as in cutting the overall out-of-pocket expenses comprising transportation, food and medication required for healthcare. The overall benefits of the HEFs were found to be helping both the poor and the ultra-poor. Additionally, Men and Pelt also highlight HEFs protective mechanisms towards indebtedness due to high costs of healthcare. Thus HEFs are also instrumental in poverty reduction, although the programme itself remains donor dependent.

In this collection, Lawson et al. have brought together a selection of contributions that highlight the adverse circumstances faced by the poorest cohorts. Each of these problems is then addressed through specific development programme and policy in the particular social and geographic context. Each selection demonstrates some shift in one or more poverty domain, helping to improve the situation of the poorest and enabling to break the poverty trap. There is acknowledgement that much remains to be done, and the challenges continue to persist. However, these case studies demonstrate that policy focus on social protection, gender empowerment and public services in particular can help the extreme poor to move out of their insecure situations. The findings further emphasize the need for a dedicated policy focus to reach the ultra-poor.

Analytical framework for identifying best practices

The search for an analytical framework that captures practices from the policy arena of anti-poverty strategies with a proven track record of successful outcomes takes us to the works of Oyen (2002) and Fosu (2013). Spanning over a decade, these studies offer two distinct approaches to analyse favourable development outcomes. Each contribution in Oyen et al.'s work first presents a conceptual engagement with the term 'best practice' and its use in the domain of poverty reduction. The theoretical constructs that emerge from these insightful epistemologically grounded argumentations are then deployed to understand a poverty reduction strategy in specific case studies with positive outcomes. Some key features that make this inquiry noteworthy are: the dynamic nature of contexts and the interventions needed, transferability of key knowledge with context specificity, the influence of actors and who should decide whether the intervention is successful and it entails 'best practices'. Cognizant of the ambiguity in the term 'best practice', Oyen defines it as a notion imbued with hope and promise of success together with a sense of it being better than something else. The success here is as per some agreed yardstick and benchmark and mostly narrated within a policy framework. This results in the 'how' of the process, key knowledge and learning from it along with how it might be applicable in different contexts to seldom remain invisible. Oyen et al. attempt to unravel and engage with the valuable information generated in the process of actioning best practices. As the first step, Oyen pushes the boundaries beyond actions that resolve and mitigate social problems and attributes innovative ideation, ways of addressing situations that enthuse others to participate and a novel approach as part of the 'best practice' milieu. Second, best practice is considered a dynamic process. This enables time-related contextual grounding by locating the change actions, the ideation and the new approaches within the society's temporal normative values. Further, Oyen draws attention to the potential pitfalls in attempts to transplant best practices from one context to another. Understanding of specific factors that facilitated the practice and identification of enabling influences in the context of application are seen as crucial in the replicability of best practice.

The argumentations then examine the interplay of vested interests and how these actors have different needs and claims on the best practice process in an increasingly donor-driven development agenda. Best practice serves to justify return on investment to the taxpayers of donor governments. The third sector needs best practice to further justify its funding and support the activities. Policymakers need best practices to maintain and expand their appeal to donors to seek more funding. Development consultants need best practice to establish their credentials and attract more projects. But who should decide a practice is *best* and against what and whose norms should it be judged? Oyen examines the dilemmas between the ideal and the actual paradigm for the selection criteria and arriving at the best practice verdict. Those who are the direct recipients of particular interventions and those who live the consequences should be the rightful owners of selection and judgement. This is seldom so. The normative foundations and yardsticks of success are more often than not crafted by a combination of agents from those running the project, the donors and the activists or the NGOs and consultants. Within the discourse of ownership of the intervention, a few minority interventions may seek insights from users and providers of the intervention to build its best practice framework. The users, though, will take the decisions based on their sphere of knowledge and information. For the poorest people this can be limited in certain domains resulting in demands for insufficient inputs and substandard services to improve their lives.

Joshi and Moore's contribution seeks generic attributes that have enabled certain programmes to perform and produce better outcomes than others. Collective action is identified as one of the most important mechanisms to allow a meaningful input of the poor and increase their influence in shaping the anti-poverty programmes. Interventions where mobilizing the collective strengths of the recipients is integral to the programme are considered strong contenders for best practice. Additionally, an enabling environment that facilitates poor people's access to public resources is also considered part of the larger best practice minutia. Miller's chapter draws attention to the complexity and intertwined nature of sociological problems in general and poverty in particular. An integrated approach to addressing poverty reduction instead of a siloed approach is therefore suggested as crucial in constructing best practice. Miller warns against direct transplantation of a practice from one context to another. Here, respect and adaptation to the values and relationships within the new landscape are noted as essential ingredients in best practice models. Cimadamore et al. situate their argumentations in two poverty reduction grassroots case studies in Argentina. The authors show the best practice to be a specific type of research evaluation tool for social programmes. The construction of this analytical framework is suggested through a structured protocol that ensures the assimilation of criteria formulated by multiple stakeholders. These include beneficiaries, researchers, policymakers and the relevant practitioners. The judgements offered by the beneficiaries are considered central in shaping the best practice selection process.

Fosu's (2013) edited collection presents a wide spectrum of global country case studies from the developing world with a proven track record of successful development strategies. Each case study is analysed for its key drivers of achievements within four fixed parameters followed by lessons learnt from each. The parameters of the analytical framework include drawing out the prefatory context that needed change, identifying the internal and external factors that shaped the strategy, outlining contributions of national and international actors and lastly articulation of the potential challenges. The country case studies are grouped into five regional clusters – East Asia and the Pacific: South Korea, Malaysia, Thailand and Vietnam; Emerging Asian Giants: India and China; sub-Saharan Africa: Botswana, Mauritius, South Africa and Ghana; Latin America and the Caribbean: Brazil, Chile, Costa Rica and the Dominican Republic; Middle-East and North

Africa: Oman/Bahrain, Tunisia and the United Arab Emirates. The focus in each contribution is a particular macro policy context of the state. In the East Asia Pacific group countries, the common features were the emphasis on (1) growth with some structural changes as being essential for development, (2) including certain distributional elements, especially inequality and poverty to growth, and (3) conceptualization of development as public good – hence it is growth combined with other social dimensions that constitute development. A key ingredient for the successful implementation of the strategic approach based on these principles is institutional building for the efficient delivery of policy.

In the Emerging Asian Giant group, other than the vastness of geographical area and the billion plus populations in each, the two countries have little in common in any other domain. With very different histories, culture, religion, language and political models, the neighbouring giants embraced domestic economic reforms, trade liberalization and restructuring of state-owned enterprises. Often these pragmatic reforms were aimed at reaching a Pareto optimum between the state and the private agents' goals and decisions. These measures resulted in active participation in global trade and international finance and banking sectors. While the state continues to be a key actor in both economies, its central role in China within the *disinterested government*[1] construct and its role within the *partial government* construct in India offer significant point of departure between the two countries. The economic strides made in both countries with positive growth rates throughout the financial crisis of 2008 continue to be of global significance. China's overall stronger performance with over 10 per cent growth dipping to 7 per cent over the last two years is attributed to its disinterested government.

Four disparate countries – Ghana, Botswana, South Africa and Mauritius – are selected for the sub-Saharan Africa group. All four countries are noted for their respective achievements and progress in the face of insurmountable challenges and predictions of the experts. The challenges were mostly sociopolitical but also geographical in the

1. Yao (Yao, 2103 in Fosu, 2013) deploys the concept of *disinterested* and *partial* governments to describe different typologies of state-constituency engagement. The former represents a government with impartial and equal dispensation to all sections of the society. The latter represents a government with special treatment and welfare prioritization of certain section of society over others.

case of Botswana and Mauritius. Ghana has crafted a path away from SSA country features of political instability, fragile growth rates with increasing debt burden and sluggish movement in poverty reduction. Its liberal reforms in the 1980s have translated into economic stability and encouraging progress in human development. Botswana's landlocked harsh terrain and the feeble attention given during the colonial era have not deterred the country from transitioning into a stable democratic state with strong economic growth. Additionally, the country's forthright leadership has steered its rich resource endowment away from the 'resource curse' trap as in many SSA countries. The small island country of Mauritius is acknowledged for delivering one of the most sustained macroeconomic stability with notable improvements in the human development indicators between 1960 and 2005. The equitable growth resulted in the country's average income to be at par with the wealthier Caribbean Islands. The continent's largest economy, South Africa was faced with an economic stagnation and downturn, a divided society, injustices and threats of being plunged into a civil war. Through peaceful negotiations between 1993 and 1994 the country's sociopolitical collapse was averted and a progressive democratic constitution was adopted. This restored the country's growth trajectory along with the implementation of a pro-poor social agenda resulting in over 3 million people being lifted out of poverty between 2000 and 2004. While each country followed a specific approach, all four embraced robust macroeconomic changes, institution building and trade reforms far more systematically than other SSA countries. Good governance is another common feature in all four countries.

The Latin America group too comprises four very diverse countries in terms of area, population and performance. Chile with just a tenth of Brazil's population is seen as the most consistent top player having a twenty-year track record of stable growth. Free market and the private sector are seen to have played a key role in the country's transition from fiscal deficits to surplus. Brazil, with forty times bigger population than Costa Rica and the biggest country in Latin America, has a tumultuous trajectory of economic reform following the end of the military rule in 1985. The country underwent a series of economic downturns despite embracing liberalization. These included worsening of debt burden, sluggish growth and crash of the currency in 1999. The same period was further noted for the sweeping privatization of all public-sector industry and utilities. Since 2003 there has been a bigger attention to the social agenda together with a stronger handle on the macroeconomic stability. These measures resulted in trade and current accounts surplus albeit over a short-lived period. Brazil has continued to be faced with tenacious fiscal problems, declining interest rates and unsustainable public debt and social spending. Improvements in the distribution of income to bring down inequality and reductions in overall poverty in Brazil though are noteworthy. Costa Rica, the oldest democracy in Latin America, embarked on institutional reforms in 1949 resulting in three decades of sustained economic growth and tangible progress in human development indicators. The 1980s was a decade of debt crisis and the subsequent negotiations and new strategies to address the debt. Costa Rica was able to secure access to international and national credit based on its robust financial management record. This enabled the protection of social expenditures while embracing tax and budgetary reforms. However, the public debt burden has burgeoned over the years restraining monetary instruments and making the country vulnerable to external shocks. The social unrests have further slowed the economic reforms. Dominican Republic adopted an export-oriented and tourism-focused development strategy in the mid-1980s that yielded strong economic indicators. This economic growth though did not bring about improvements in social development, and public spending in critical domains of health and education remained low. The structural adjustment reforms of the 1990s spurred the miracle growth in the country between 1996 and 2000 that was rapidly squandered in the political regime between 2000 and 2004. Since 2004 policy focus to regain the lost progress and restore stability was adopted with the support of the IMF. Despite these measures along with high levels of inward foreign investment, the export growth remains feeble with slowdown in the GDP growth and weakened competitiveness. While the four countries in the Latin American group exhibit significant differences, Cardoso (2013 in Fosu, 2013) observes three key themes that are present in each country. These include income inequality, export of natural resources and its impact on development and macroeconomic stabilization following long periods of financial disarray.

The MENA region countries are bound by a shared history and a common cultural heritage. Home to the world's biggest oil reserves in the modern times, the region also boasts of prosperity and economic supremacy between seventh to the thirteenth centuries. Since the mid-twentieth century though, resource endowments and management of resource-related incomes show wide variations among the twenty-one nations that occupy the region. Within oil price volatility induced economic instabilities, three of the four selected countries in Fosu's edited collection demonstrate good management of oil revenues.

Bahrain and Oman achieved strong overall progress through a more equitable distribution of oil incomes and social investment to achieve social cohesion. UAE's modernization success is attributed to economic openness along with importation of skilled professionals and overseas investment of surplus oil revenues into sovereign wealth funds. Tunisia, the fourth country in the group with far limited resources than the other three, demonstrates yet another route to achieving sustained economic growth. Hailed as a success story by the IMF, Tunisia embarked on IMF and the World Bank supported economic reforms to strengthen its export-oriented manufacturing sector. Further the country has experienced relative political stability, engaged with economic diversification in trade, has a highly educated skilled labour force and fostered women's empowerment. These four countries offer insights into the different approaches to economic and social development in the MENA region. The key drivers of success are identified as economic freedoms, egalitarian distribution of wealth to create public goods and services with overall good management of resources.

How to bring about change?

There is rich literature on social change. The focus in this section though is to capture *how* social change happens at both micro and macro levels. This resonates with the views found in the Marxian discourse that urge social theory to go beyond interpretation and understanding of the society to showing new ways of doing things and driving change. Within the domain of international development, emergence of the conceptual engagement with the 'theory of change' paradigm in the mid-1990s ushered a discreet focus on processes that connect actions with the desired outcomes. In a comprehensive review of the Theory of Change (ToC) in international development, Stein and Valters (2012) draw attention to its origins in the evaluation methodologies for community initiatives in United States in the early 1990s. Its usage in the development arena is further shaped by how the logical planning framework approach introduced in the 1970s influenced evaluation and also by the practitioners' quest for theoretically informed practice to bring social change. The latter can be traced to the emergence of participatory approaches that urged reflection and synthesis of development theory for informed action a decade earlier in the 1960s. While consensus on the precise definitions of ToC remains elusive as noted by Stein and Valter, a handful of studies offer insightful building blocks. Starting with Weiss's (Weiss, 1995) conception of ToC as a 'theory of how and why an initiative works', the idea is further spelt out by Davies (2012), 'the description of a sequence of events that is expected to lead to a particular desired outcome' and elaborated by Rodgers (2008), 'Every programme is packed with beliefs, assumptions and hypotheses about how change happens – about the way humans work, or organisations, or political systems, or eco-systems. Theory of change is about articulating these many underlying assumptions about how change will happen in a programme.'

Vogel (2012, p. 8) attributes the mainstreaming of ToC approach in recent years to three key drivers. These include, first, the ever-increasing demands for evidence-based results to show impact as well as the transparency required to justify decision making. Second, the need to capture the complexities and uncertainties anchored in the political and social contexts that surround the development domain. Further, ToC not only enables awareness of the complexities that underpin the development dynamics but also offers ways of facing and resolving these challenges. Finally, acknowledgement of context specificity and country ownership of development programmes is increasingly recognized as the cornerstone of development cooperation and country support by donors. This entails engaging and collaborating with local actors, institutions and their capacities together with their up-skilling if so required. ToC approach allows mapping of these relationships, contexts, activities and impacts.

The mainstreaming of ToC has led to its adoption as the key-planning tool for understanding change, achieving outcomes, facilitating progress and mapping impact by a wide range of institutions. These include civil society organizations, NGOs, donor agencies – bilateral and multilateral, think tanks/consultants and evaluation agencies. The multiple applicability of ToC though can be problematic as noted by Stein and Valters (p 6). While it lends itself to be deployed in unlimited forms with different contents, these are often presented as a schema capturing the pathways to outcomes located in the specific micro and macro contexts. Representation of complexity is achieved through mostly complicated diagrams that can be arduous to interpret and difficult to engage with. In his 'From Poverty to Power' blog, Duncan Green (2012b) comments on the perils of this complexity by the possibility of putting off or 'terrifying' some users. Green suggests doing away with the schemas as *toolkits* once the initial scenario replication and activity outcome pathways have been crafted. Instead, he favours its use as an enabler for 'ToC thinking' as distinct from a mechanical ToC tick boxing exercise drawing example from the practices developed by the Dutch NGO Hivos.

The ToC thinking can be seen as offering one of the critical foundation stones for facilitating the desired change. Duncan Green (2016, p. 28) brings to attention the centrality and critical role of power in initiating and in achieving change. His entry into the power discourse in international development is through the copiously used concept of *empowerment*, which is the bedrock of the human development paradigm shaped by Amartya Sen (1999). Within a people-centred approach to development, Sen defined development as the expansion of opportunities and freedoms and a process that facilitates what people value doing and being. Empowerment thus became the driving force to enable human development as per this approach. Green further notes that engagement with notions of power, from which the origins of empowerment are derived, though, remains thin within the international development arena.

Various constructs of the power dynamics can be traced to the Foucauldian conceptions of power as the ability to change behaviour of individuals or to bring about change – positive or negative in the society. Further, power can also be positive or negative. It is amorphous and relational located in multiple sources rather than exclusively negative and the remit of a few individuals or institutions. Luke's dimensions of power, such as visible, hidden and invisible (Luke, 1974) –further advanced by Rowlands (1997); VeneKlasen and Miller (2002) and Gaventa (2006) – draw on some of Foucault's optimistic concepts. These constructs offer a more direct and structured engagement to facilitate change by addressing the manifestations of the three forms of power in a community. Thus, interventions are identified to strengthen power: *within* – self-confidence and awareness of entitlements; *with* – power through finding common ground and building collective strength; *to* – opportunity to achieve and shape one's life; and *over* – the traditional hierarchical power entailing domination, force, coercion and decision-making authority with a win–lose relationship. This categorization into four expressions of power captures three positive typologies of power (*within*, *with* and *to*) and one negative (*over*), demonstrating the Foucauldian explication of power comprising both positive and negative dimensions. Amidst scattered, albeit emerging literature locating the power discourse within the development landscape, its role in both impeding and enabling progress is undisputed.

Green (2016) further draws attention to a few other key actors that have a critical role in initiating and influencing change. The most important of these is the state with rich literature to support the centrality of its position and leadership in steering change. The re-emergence of this well-founded narrative began at the end of the twentieth century with Chang and Rowthorn's (1995) publication on the role of state in economic change and which has expanded into the twenty-first century with a wider audience. There was a backlash against the state following decades of slow progress and failures in the developing countries during the 1960s and 1970s. The developed countries also experienced stiff rejection of the welfare state during the same period. These events resulted in the embrace and spread of the market-driven agenda in the 1980s and the collapse of the state central planning symbolized by the fall of the Berlin Wall in 1989. The euphoria though was short lived as pointed by Chang and Rowthorn (1995). Based on ten contributions that examine both state interventionism and neoliberal anti-interventionism in a range of country contexts, they warn off the misleading arguments of neoliberalism. A search for a new narrative that captures the valid aspects of neoliberalism combined with the role of state, located within specific cultural and institutional contexts, is suggested.

Ha-Joon Chang's focus on the role of state in the development of a country remains a key thematic strand in his subsequent works (2001a, 2001b, 2002, 2003, 2008). Amongst the other copious array of research that emerged on the theme, Lockwood (2005) and Green (2008) in particular dwell into inquiring how the state can initiate, shape and sustain change. Matthew Lockwood offers evidence-based powerful argumentation for placing the lion's share of decades of development failures in the African nations on weak states, poor governance and clientelism. The central theme of Lockwood's work is the focus on political reforms to enable the creation of developmental states as seen in its emergence in Botswana, Ghana and Mozambique, for example. The problems with the flawed international engagement in Africa seem much less than those engendered by weak states. Progressive change in Africa, poverty eradication in particular, would be addressed far better through effective states. Duncan Green's emphasis is on the ability of effective states to change the world. He provides an insightful theoretical understanding of the modern state in terms of an institution that is charged with the responsibility of the welfare of its citizens by ensuring their security, creating opportunities, offering social protection and guaranteeing the rights and voices of all sections of the society. Green, however, alerts to the gulf between 'the what should be' theoretical conceptualization to the reality, rampant with state as the mechanism to protect the interests of the elites. This should not deter the active citizen to channel their efforts and involvement towards creating and supporting an effective and accountable state that respects non-state actors.

An individual-focused analysis of how to change the world where certain people at the grassroots are drivers of change in the society is found in the work of David Bornstein (2007). Bornstein chronicles a series of untold stories of individuals whose ideas have improved and made a tangible difference in the lives of multitudes of people. Spread across both developed and developing countries from the United States, South Africa, Poland, India, Hungary, Brazil and Bangladesh, the only common attribute they share is their new ideas to address social problems and the relentless pursuit of their goals. He calls these individuals social entrepreneurs. Bornstein is quick, though, to distinguish between the thematic core of social entrepreneurship that is rapidly gaining popularity amidst a wide range of audience and the take on social entrepreneur in his investigation. These micro actors are viewed as transformative forces that embody Jean-Baptise Say's characterization of entrepreneur as a *special economic actor*, Schumpeter's *creative destruction* and Peter Drucker's notions of *ability to change the capacity of a society*. The selected examples in the book demonstrate that social change can often be traced to a single individual. This individual sees the societal problems, envisions a solution and through his/her sheer grit, unwavering determination and belief drives the innovation needed to tackle the problem. The process requires gathering support to harness collective power, raising resources, advocacy and building an institution. Albeit small at the start, such institutions help channel the resources and effort, provide the energy and encouragement needed to overcome resistance along with a range of other impediments.

Bornstein further observes that for the previous combination of positive factors to coalesce into a force that propels novel ways of resolving the most chronic social problems, freedoms to access opportunities as well as material resources are essential. Post-colonial and post-dictatorships era of more openness and freedoms coupled with technological advancements have ushered in the emergence of Bornstein's *citizenship sector*. While the membership of this sector is not new, comprising organizations under the historical umbrella of the 'non-profit' or 'non-governmental' or the 'third-sector', the scale of its spread worldwide in terms of mobilizing citizens, forging partnerships with state, private sector and academia together with the employment growth in the sector is new. Not surprisingly, there is also an increase in the use of the sector as a respectable facade for the corrupt and dubious practices by numerous organizations. This has led to the erosion of trust to some extent and hence the requirements for greater transparency and need to demonstrate impact and efficacy.

Additionally, wider elements at the global level that have espoused citizens' understandings of the problems in their immediate spheres as well as in the wider connected world include access to information, communication tools and ability to link with like-minded people. The challenges include the awareness, on the one hand, of the huge strides made in the last fifty years in human longevity, education, health and women's rights,[2] while, on the other, deepening economic and social inequalities and environmental destruction pose widening insecurities.[3] A few members of the citizenship sector are social innovators and take it upon themselves to find solutions to social problems through inspiring, gathering, coordinating and driving collective effort.

Bornstein identifies another genre of actors in the citizenship sector without whose contribution the social entrepreneurs' path to success would be far more formidable and gruelling. He uses the example of Bill Drayton, the founder of the organization Ashoka, which had financially supported over 1,800 social entrepreneurs across the globe by 2007. As early as 1988, the organization created a social-action blueprint repository – picked from a rich source, comprising over 1,000 entries from 94 countries – of examples of progress being made in access to clean water, affordable housing, conflict resolution and environmental protection. Very early on it became obvious to the organization that for most social entrepreneurs, achieving financial sustainability was perhaps the toughest hurdle. A financial compatriot of the social-action blueprint was subsequently created through Citizen Base Initiative. First, this identified individuals, who had attained some degree of local support and reduced dependence on external sources. These resource-mobilization strategies were then analysed and collated into a good

2. Average global life expectancy has more than doubled from 29 years in the early nineteenth century to 66 years by the early twenty-first century with sharp increases in the developing world in the last century – 35.6 years in 1950 to 50.5 years in Africa, 28 years in 1900 to 67.1 years in 2001 in Asia, Riley (2005).

3. Global adult literacy increased from 76 per cent to 86 per cent between 1990 and 2011, while in developing countries it went up from 64 per cent to 80 per cent in the same period UNESCO (2013).

practice handbook for making it available to those starting up on the financing of their social innovation.

The rationale for the creation of this unique repository of social innovation strategies and its financing models is grounded in Ashoka's conviction that the most impactful social innovations start with individuals who are dispersed and mostly resource constrained. Bornstein further notes the organization's observation of the expanding pool of novel problem solving with origins outside of the state, the academia or other structured institutions. Ashoka strives to support these individual social innovators and capture their collective knowledge to enable numerous fledgling ideas to attain their potential to address a community problem and be up scaled.

How development progress has happened

The Overseas Development Institute (ODI) initiated the Development Progress Project (DPP) in 2011 to map the positive outcomes of development efforts at the global level. Based on evidence from twenty-five case studies[4] located in different sectors spread across the global south, the project aimed to capture what development intervention has worked, why it has worked and how it can be measured. An important driver for this project is noted as the need to be cognizant of more progress made in key development domains since the 1990s than in any other time in history. The achievements are even more noteworthy given the complexity of the ever-increasing global challenges and despite the failures of development often dominating development news.

DPP's '10 Things to know about International Development' (ODI, 2016) highlights ten exemplars from fifty case studies situated in countries that have attained remarkable milestones in a range of domains. These include near elimination of extreme poverty in *Vietnam* between 1993 and 2012 by lifting just over 60 per cent of the country's population living under $1.25 PPP (2005) prices out of poverty by 2012. This was made possible by investment in social infrastructure and market opportunities, modernization of agriculture and boost in productivity along with trade reforms that protected domestic interest

4. The second phase of the project has added another twenty-five, producing in all a series of fifty case studies from which to draw on what different countries have done to achieve development progress in recent years.

– *Nepal's* remarkable reduction in maternal mortality from 901 to 258 per 100,000 live births between 1990 and 2015. This was made possible by substantial increase in the government spending in health expenditure from $34 to $66 per person between 1995 and 2010 and significant improvements in access to maternal healthcare services free of cost in both urban and rural areas. In addition, women's educational levels as well as incomes have risen steadily while fertility has fallen; *Kenya's* efforts in up-skilling its youth beyond basic education resulted in secondary school enrolment from 40 per cent to 67 per cent between 2000 and 2012, and doubling of enrolment in public universities between 2007–8 and 2012–13. This was made possible through a combination of state, non-state and citizens' interventions. The public spending in education was increased by over 40 per cent between 2003–4 and 2010–11. It was channelled through decentralized mechanisms for infrastructure improvements and expansion in bursary provision. Further, with the introduction of free primary education following the election pledge, over a million additional children went to school in 2003. Secondary education was made free in 2008. Two other factors were at play during the same period. First, with far more children completing primary and secondary education, the demand for higher education was triggered not just from the students but also from the employers who raised their skill requirements. Second, the newly created space for education provision across the primary, secondary and university levels has attracted a wide range of non-state providers. These included the faith-based schools and private institutions, thus further expanding the educational opportunities; urban poverty in the slums of *Peru* declined by more than half in the twelve-year period between 2001 and 2013. This was made possible by the government's large investments in service improvements in the slums along with extensive programmes for housing provision and title deeds. The outcomes were given a boost and reinforced through community action and negotiations with the state to improve services. The inhabitants further advanced their housing situations by drawing on their social capital and their own labour to invest and build houses. *Burkina Faso's* successes in sustainable agricultural practices have led to regaining large areas of degraded land for farming thus strengthening food security and reducing income insecurity. These practices have also helped in mitigating the adverse impacts of climate change on agriculture. The outcomes were made possible by drawing on the farmers' local knowledge to develop appropriate technological interventions, extensive engagement with the communities, and the civic society with a strong financial backing from the state. *Tunisia* stands out in the Arab world for its progressive policy focus for the advancement of women's rights through access and improvements in healthcare provision for women, their education, employment and political representation. These measures weathered the Arab Spring with further improvements in women's position such that they occupy a third of the current Parliament. These achievements have been made possible through a strong political will to build an inclusive secular state with emphasis on gender equality and women's empowerment. The reforms within this agenda included expansion of education and paid employment opportunities for women. These in turn fortified their reproductive rights and collective strengths. The women's invigorated collective agency resulted in wider public debate on gender equality and their participation in shaping policy at the state level; the FS of *Timor-Leste*, with its recent history of a violent civil war, is noted for the huge improvements in the safety of its citizens accompanied by a tangible reduction in politically motivated violence. This was made possible by a combination of internal and external factors working together. A functioning coalition government since almost a decade has led to political stability and control over violent unrest and security. Burgeoning petroleum-based revenues have enabled the state to channel resources towards improving public services. In addition, the state has also embarked on a 'one-off peace payment' and support to return to civilian life to the former adversaries. *Sri Lanka's* efforts since the early 2000 despite the severe setbacks of the 2004 tsunami, as well as decades of conflict and civil war, have resulted in a drastic fall in unemployment to just 4 per cent by 2012. While the overall quality of jobs has been of a good standard (the output per worker went up from \$10,460 in 1992 to \$21,587-PPP, 2011 prices, ODI, 2016; p. 18), the employment expansion has been more for women, thus helping to reduce the proportion of working poor by half in just under ten years (between 2005 and 2014). This has been made possible by the unique stance of the government to promote pro-market reforms along with prioritizing employment opportunities in the public sector. Further, significant increases in the FDI in the manufacturing for export created yet more jobs. Other enabling policies included supplementing the already high literacy with technical and vocational inputs, leading to trebling of people with higher technical and vocational skills in just under a decade (between 2005 and 2014). In addition, the large proportion of Sri Lankan migrants working overseas has helped in both the high levels of remittances accounting almost 8 per cent of the GDP in 2010 and keeping the job market free from over supply. *Ecuador's* phenomenal progress in reducing income inequality between 2006 and 2011 is an example of how tenacious roots of inequality can be weakened. The country is credited for achieving one of the most inclusive economic growths globally spurring the incomes of the country's poorest 40 per cent to grow eight times more than the national average during the same period. Thus, between 2000 and 2012 while the average national wage increased by 75 per cent the wages of the bottom quartile increased by 140 per cent (ODI, 2016; p. 20). This was made possible by the government's priority focus on pro-poor policies in both economic and social domains. Social policy reforms included increase in social expenditure from one of the lowest in Latin America in 2000 (2.9 per cent of GDP) to 8.3 per cent by 2012, direct cash transfers to the poorest households and removal of barriers to health services and education. The pro-poor economic policy focus comprised gaining stability by adopting conservative fiscal tools of low taxes with liberalization but channelling revenues from a buoyant oil market to expand opportunities in sectors employing the poorest labour. These measures were also accompanied by the state-supported financing of social redistributive policies. *Ethiopia* is considered the star of East Africa's development landscape as a result of its remarkable achievements in multiple domains over the last two decades. The country has undergone the steepest fall in extreme poverty at the global level with decreasing unemployment and halving of the informal sector workforce between 1999 and 2000. It is on track to achieve universal enrolment in primary education while keeping a handle on inequality. This has been made possible by the comprehensive implementation of the government's overarching goal of poverty reduction and to reach middle-income country status by 2025. It has entailed highly pro-poor focused strategies in both the social and economic arenas. Ethiopia's social protection programme covering over 1.5 million people is the largest in Africa, and 70 per cent of its capital spending is directed to five service sectors most used by the poor – education, health, water supply, transport and agriculture. The country has benefited hugely from its double-digit growth of 11 per cent for over a decade, spurring private-sector-supported investment in rural infrastructure, agricultural training and job creation in the wider economy.

DPP (ODI, 2016; p.24) points to the relevance of context specificity in how countries can overcome problems of poverty and make progress for all its people, but identifies six factors that recur in most of the fifty case studies examined. The ten exemplars, in particular, demonstrate that these drivers with adaptations, if needed, are essential for achieving positive change. *Political leadership* scores the highest in the essential drivers for development to work scorecard. Having a vision and a policy is not sufficient; it is also important to have a political will and direction for resource mobilization, collaboration and implementation. *Effective policies* that encompass reforms to reinvigorate economic growth, while targeting the needs of the most vulnerable in the society, are needed to enable inclusive development. *Institutional capacity* is essential to foster accountability and governance in the society. States need ring-fenced and guaranteed *finance* flows to fund public services instead of placing the burden on the poor households. Contributions made through sound *donor partnerships* using the official development assistance pledge to support infrastructure building and facilitating political stability are significant. Lastly, participation of citizens through *collective action* in demanding and engaging with service provision was seen in most of the case studies. The report concludes by alerting to the plight of the most marginalized households that continue to be left behind but draws attention and hope to the SDGs focus on 'leave no one behind'.

So, what can we learn from the story so far?

In the seven decades since the establishment of the Bretton Woods institutions to oversee rebuilding of the global economy, and support nation building in the poorer countries, the development progress story has undergone a roller-coaster trajectory. There have been huge failures but there have been successes too. One example of disappointing outcomes of development interventions is hunger-related deaths and health setbacks each year. The hunger statistics of the World Food Programme (WFP, 2016) indicates one in nine (795 million) people on earth who do not have enough food to lead healthy and active life; nearly half of deaths in children under five (3.1 million) are caused by poor nutrition each year; the number of hungry could be reduced by up to 150 million if women farmers had the same resources as men; 66 million primary school-age children attend classes hungry across the developing world. During the same period, however, achievement in adult literacy is a success story example.

Five of the seven decades of the post-Bretton Woods are succinctly summarized by Elson (1997). The first two decades were ruled by industrialization followed by a somewhat feeble and short-lived wealth redistribution and basic needs agenda. It was the 1980s that saw the return of the market approach with vengeance followed by complete dominance of the financial-criteria-led development within a neoliberal rubric. The fifth decade in the 1990s ushered in some hope and an upward trajectory in the development narrative with a bigger attention to human-centred development. It certainly lasted up to 2008 with widespread buoyant debates on the achievement of the MDGs, and the OECD member countries pledge to meet the 0.7 per cent ODA commitment. The seventh decade since Bretton Woods has seen the slippage of the relatively benign period development agenda directed at the poorer regions of the world following the financial crises of 2008[5] once again faced the onslaught of budget cuts and its existence questioned in some quarters.

The key themes that emerge from good practices and achievements in the efforts towards improving the lives of the poor living in developing countries are located in both macro and micro domains. The success stories at the micro level not always link up with the macro framework of the state, as illustrated by the examples in Veit et al. (1995). Yet, they are critical in the overall progress in the betterment of human lives. The CBAs to development in the post-SAP period of the 1980s shaped numerous micro experiments comprising sustainable development activities throughout Africa. Driven by individuals and communities, many of these initiatives included sustainable development activities enabling the use of collective strengths, local knowledge, local resource and its conservation for future generations. However, much of these success stories remained masked under the dismal macro development outcomes of the post-SAPs era as noted by Veit et al. (1995). There was feeble integration of these projects into the national plans, and there was no framework for adoption and scaling-up. Thus, 'Lessons from ground up' despite robust evidence of positive outcomes did not influence the top-down macro policy focus in Africa. In the case of the AKRSP for the Siddi community in Gir Forest in Gujarat starting in the 1980s, the socially excluded tribal community has made tangible progress. The AKRSP identified specific needs of the Siddis and multiple domains that needed to be strengthened for this marginalized cohort to

5. ODA decline to least developing countries.

https://www.theguardian.com/global-development/2015/apr/08/foreign-aid-spending-2014-least-developed-countries

https://oecdinsights.org/2015/04/13/how-the-world-reacted-to-the-latest-aid-data/

break the shackles of intergenerational hopelessness and acceptance of their deprived circumstances. Such targeted interventions are possible and far more effective within a micro setting instead of a generic macro framework. Albeit, tapping into the existing social policy for improving the socio-economic contexts of the tribals and accessing their entitlements was crucial in the positive outcomes. Thus, while this micro experiment was not scaled up, it certainly connected with the existing relevant macro policy framework.

While the macro domains mostly fall within the remit of the state, some large third-sector players also engage with interventions at macro level. State-led successes indicate an active role of the governments in tackling a development domain that is adversely impacting the lives of the poor. Thus, the Government of Cambodia's recognition and efforts to finance healthcare provision in a highly under-resourced health sector have resulted in a much-improved healthcare access by poor and the poorest. The measures implemented in partnership with the third sector included reducing health-related poverty and expanding health service utilization by the poor through Health Equity Fund. Since its first pilot in 2000, the partnership with the third sector continues, albeit with a far more 'hands on' involvement of the state.

Another state-led macro experiment is India's flagship public works programme NREGA, launched in 2005. It builds on India's long-standing policy tradition in public works through cash transfer to the poorest to mitigate their worsening circumstances in times of distress and emergencies. NREGA's initial success includes cash transfer to the most needy to stall the downward spiral of poverty, though problems of leakages, poor targeting, lack of accountability and unsuitable asset creation loom over NREGA. In addition, its plans to include the priorities of the communities in asset building ran aground due to mostly poor participation by women and feeble capacity of the village institutions.

The third sector-led macro interventions indicate a sharp focus and a deeper engagement with the specific poverty dimension but still requiring a wide range of social and economic policy context for transformative change to take place. Oxfam GB's 'just giving cash' in Vietnam and BRAC's TUP programme in Bangladesh illustrate this point. The one-off unconditional cash transfer to 500 BPL households in 8 villages in Ha Tinh province of Vietnam was situated within the hypothesis that the poor themselves prioritize their own needs best and direct the money to address these requirements responsibly. The research showed that such unconditional cash transfers should be viewed as one of the means to help the poorest households to move away from the downward spiral of poverty. The opportunity expansion requires a wide spectrum of social and economic provisions.

The TUP was also focused on reaching the poorest people in Bangladesh and helping them to break away from the poverty trap through asset and skill building. It captured the 25–30 million ultra-poor people who had remained untouched by the remarkable progress made by the country by 2004. Within a multidimensional underpinning of poverty, TUP adopted specific targeting strategies to reach the ultra-poor in different domains. Analysis of this experiment shows that this specificity in targeting and mapping programmes to a particular poverty dimension was possible because of BRAC's established expertise and professional capacity to administer programmes. While such customization of strategies to poverty produces overall positive shifts in the lives of the poorest, the processes are highly resource- and skill-intensive. Further, again it was within a progressive pro-poor social policy context that TUP operationalized its strategies many of which linked with the existing services.

There is yet another successful intervention sphere as seen in Chile's anti-poverty social assistance programme *Chile Solidario* launched in 2002. The social macro policy context and the micro grassroots actors are closely integrated. Within this integrated approach, a number of context-specific programme as per the self-identified needs of the poorest in the domains of education, health, childcare and unforeseen setbacks along with the direct monetary transfer are combined. Another novel feature of the project is its focus on enhancing the agency of the poorest households through access to opportunities, information and participation.

Successful development can also be captured through analytical frameworks that gauge indicators and proxies for epistemologically arrived definitions of *positive outcomes of development*. Two such examples by Oyen (2002) and Fosu (2013) demonstrate distinct approaches to analyse favourable development outcomes. The former unravels the 'how' of the process in different contexts to achieve progress through a milieu of practices. Some noteworthy features include pushing the boundaries beyond actions that resolve social problems to include innovative ideation and ways that enthuse others to participate as part of the 'best practice' pathway to progress. Additionally, the potential pitfalls in ignoring context specificity, the interplay of vested interests and the ownership of the intervention in terms of judging if the outcome is positive are other crucial factors that shape the framework.

Contributions in Oyen's work highlight further important drivers. These include mobilizing collective strengths, an enabling environment that facilitates poor people's access to public resources, an integrated approach instead of a siloed approach to addressing poverty and criteria formulated by multiple stakeholders. The judgements offered by the beneficiaries are considered central in shaping the best practice selection process.

While Oyen et al. offer ways of identifying micro and macro best practices, Fosu's analytical framework uses four fixed parameters to construct a largely macro policy-focused tool. These parameters are drawing out the precise prefatory context that need change, identifying the internal and external factors that shape strategy, outlining contributions of national and international actors and lastly articulation of the potential challenges. Country case studies examined within this framework in five regional clusters – East Asia and the Pacific, Emerging Asian Giants, sub-Saharan Africa, Latin America and the Caribbean, Middle-East and North Africa – highlight the following key insights into the macro policy successes. Functioning institutions are shown to be essential for the efficient delivery of policy. The state is a key actor in the progress trajectory within both the disinterested government construct as in China and the partial government construct as in India. Macroeconomic changes along with trade reforms and a strong social agenda that benefit the domestic context and good governance are other important features. The MENA region successes further point to the economic freedoms, egalitarian distribution of wealth to create public goods with good management of resources as key drivers for their achievements.

In addition to the successful interventions and strategies deployed to achieve them, as discussed earlier, there is another domain comprising a cluster of emerging discourses that are shaping development outcomes. The first of these themes is the engagement with the theory of how and why initiatives work. The widespread embracing of the ToC has led to its adoption as the key-planning tool for understanding change, achieving outcomes, facilitating progress and mapping impact by a wide range of development institutions. These include civil society organizations, NGOs, donor agencies – bilateral and multilateral – think tanks/consultants and evaluation agencies. While ToC comprehensively captures the complexity of development contexts, the complicated schemas it relies as its building blocks can often appear daunting for those new to it. In recent literature, Green (2012a, 2016) suggest using ToC as a means to achieving the end, that is, the desired change. ToC is not the end goal; instead, it offers one of the critical foundation stones for facilitating the desired outcome. Engagement with the discourse on power remains sparse in international development despite its centrality and critical role in initiating and achieving change. However, the concept of empowerment which draws its origins from notions of power is the bedrock of the human development paradigm shaped by Amartya Sen (Sen, 1999). Within definitions of development as the expansion of opportunities and freedoms and a process that facilitates what people value doing and being, empowerment is seen as one of the key mechanisms of achieving it.

While a full-on engagement with power analysis is somewhat thin in international development, Foucauldian conceptions of power as the ability to change behaviour of individuals or to bring about change – positive or negative – are the basis for its emergence in development arena. Drawing on some of Foucault's optimistic concepts, attempts by Luke, Gaventa and others offer constructs for a more direct and structured engagement to facilitate change by addressing the different manifestations of power in a community. Amidst scattered, albeit emerging literature locating the power discourse within the development landscape, its role in both impeding and enabling progress is undisputed. Amongst other key actors in the power dynamics that affect development the state is considered the most important one. Grounded in rich literature, Green (2016) points to the centrality of its position and leadership in steering change within successes in the past and the current period. While there exist huge discrepancies between *what should be* and *what is*, the state is an institution charged with the responsibility of the welfare of its citizens. This includes ensuring their security, creating opportunities, offering social protection and guaranteeing the rights and voices of all sections of the society. Further, the gulf between the ideal and the reality should not deter citizens to channel their participation towards creating and supporting an effective and accountable state that respects non-state actors.

Another emerging theme shaping development outcomes is recognition of the critical role of micro actors. These are the individuals whose ideas have improved and made a tangible difference in the lives of multitudes of people. Bornstein's (2007) social entrepreneurs exhibit distinct features of transformative force by spotting the societal problems, ideating a solution and through their sheer determination and belief, drive the innovation needed to tackle the problem. The process requires gathering support to harness collective power, raising resources, advocacy and building an institution. Albeit small at the start, such institutions help channel the resources and effort, provide the energy and encouragement needed to overcome resistance along with a range of other impediments. Further, over the three decades or so, technological advancements combined with more openness and freedoms have led to the emergence of Bornstein's *citizenship sector.* While the membership of this sector is not new, comprising organizations under the historical umbrella of the 'non-profit' or 'non-governmental' or the 'third-sector', the scale of its spread worldwide in terms of mobilizing citizens, forging partnerships with state, private sector and academia together with the employment growth in the sector is new.

The final theme within the cluster of discourses shaping development considered in this book emerges from evidence-based investigation aimed to capture what development intervention has worked, why it has worked and how it can be measured. The ODI's DPP, launched in 2011 to map the positive outcomes of development efforts at the global level, offers insightful findings. While attention to context specificity is considered crucial in designing interventions for the desired change, DPP identifies a set of factors that recur in most of the fifty case studies examined in its research. The ten best performers, exemplars of development progress in particular, demonstrate these drivers to be essential, albeit with the necessary adaptations, for achieving positive change. These essential drivers include *political leadership*, *effective policies*, *institutional capacity*, *finance*, *donor partnerships* and *collective action* in demanding and engaging with service provision.

The macro policy realm remains dominant in influencing development progress as per the findings of the DPP research. However, political buy-in, cross-sector collaboration and community involvement are noted as vital ingredients for progress in specific case studies on global health progress. This multi-stakeholder approach has not yet been translated into a policy instrument for scaling-up or a lessons learned policy toolkit. There is increasing attention, though, being drawn to multi-stakeholder input in the DPP (ODI, 2014c). Further, the most marginalized households appear to remain untouched by the policy context and continue to be left behind. The SDGs focus on 'leave no one behind' therefore offers hope for a more inclusive development paradigm.

We need to be cognizant of more progress made in key development domains since the 1990s than in any other time in history. The achievements are even more noteworthy given the complexity of the ever-increasing global challenges and despite the failures of development often dominating development news. This itself is a strong rationale to further investigate why some development works and go beyond what the story so far tells us. These insights could offer ways of addressing the plight of the most marginalized and those caught up in the quagmire of complex problems.

Chapter 3

THE CONVERGENCE FRAMEWORK (CF)

INSIGHTS INTO WHAT MAKES SOME INTERVENTIONS ACHIEVE BETTER OUTCOMES THAN OTHERS

This chapter will present the CF developed from previous research of the author. Perceptions of poverty at the grassroots together with drivers of development will then be examined to understand how these impact actor engagement within the CF. The chapter will aim to offer insights into what makes some interventions achieve better outcomes than others – what makes development successful, not so successful or a failure

A slow-moving queue meandered in the daytime hustle of a village in Bodh Gaya in Bihar, India. The men and women in the queue each carried large hard plastic containers or large aluminium pots with exteriors blackened from soot. Frequently, the order was being disrupted with some wanting to jump the queue, leading to cacophony of commotion. The sharp voices of two women clearly in command would restore the queue every time, temporarily crush the chaos and continue with the patrol. The destination of the queue was towards two fifty-litre metal drums painted from outside to hide the corrosive rust. The drums were perched on a brick platform in an open space fully occupied with sixty to seventy curious onlookers. Next to the drums were another two women. The first of these women was checking the card the queue occupants were showing her and calling out the name to her colleague. The second woman was putting a tick against the name of those presenting their card and entering the number 2 or 3 in the next column in a ledger. The cardholder was then turning to a man who would pour a transparent liquid from the big drums into the cardholder's container using a one-litre plastic mug. Another man stood by ensuring the correct quantity of the liquid as called out by the woman to be dispensed to each customer. Amidst the sporadic pandemonium created by booming voices of men volunteering to read the cards faster, to hasten the ledger entry and to maintain order, then occasionally being snapped by the women, the queue inched on. This was operation '*PDS kerosene oil*' under a new dealership in the village.

PDS kerosene oil

The PDS (public distribution system) is India's oldest anti-poverty programme with ring-fenced budgetary expenditures at both the central and the state levels (Raghavan, 1999). Traced to the country's food crisis of the mid-1960s, it was launched as a price-supported rationing tool embedded in a strong subsidy-based food distribution programme. It included the distribution of wheat, rice, sugar and kerosene oil accessed at the Fair Price Shops (FPS) on presentation of ration cards issued to households on application to the local administration. The PDS has since then attracted much debate and criticism, with the country's position transitioning from severe food grain deficit to that of surplus. It has been revamped and expanded several times to improve its reach to cover the poorest households via the Targeted PDS (TPDS) and the Antyodaya Anna Yojna (AAY). The AAY cardholders are the ultra-poor households that qualify for further price subsidy in the grain prices.

Given that India continues to be home to one of the largest numbers of undernourished people (194.6 million) in the world (FAO, 2015), the PDS remains highly relevant, albeit contested on numerous grounds. Svedberg (2012) argues that the outcomes for the two key objectives of the PDS – to improve food security and nutrition and reduce poverty – have been quite disappointing. Based on the share of poor households in possession of the BPL ration card that allows subsidized grain purchase of 35 kilogram/month and the actual purchase by these households, the monetary subsidy was Rs.30 (approximately £25) per household in 2004–5. The underutilization of the full-grain allowance has been largely due to targeting errors and inferior grain quality. Svedberg's (2012) study further indicates that almost two-thirds (63 per cent) of the poor households did not have access to the PDS ration, and over 60 per cent of all the cards that give entitlements to the PDS were owned by the non-poor. Additionally, almost 54 per cent of the total grain allocated for PDS never reached the designated outlets where the poor could procure the grain as per the investigation carried out by the Planning Commission of India in 2008. This leakage appears to be on an upward trend between the 1993 and 1994, 1999 and 2000 and 2004 and 2005 estimates.

PDS leakage is the quantity of grain released by the Food Corporation of India to be distributed at subsidized prices that never reaches the consumers. Several inquiries into this domain reveal corruption, thefts at different levels of the distribution chain, misappropriation of PDS commodities by the FPS licensees and rent-seeking behaviour of ruling politicians (Svedberg, 2012). Dreze and Khera (2015), using the India Human Development Survey and the National Sample Survey (NSS), show notable improvement in PDS leakages in states that embraced comprehensive PDS reforms such as Bihar, Odisha and Chattisgarh. Bihar, in particular, stands out both for undertaking significant reforms and for the resulting outcomes in terms of improved grain quality and consistency of distribution. Until 2004–5, the PDS in Bihar was known for leakages between 80 and 90 per cent, with high levels of fraud and misappropriation. Despite some reductions in the leakage and better availability of PDS grain, the PDS in Bihar remained one of the most corrupt in the country. Tangible signs of improvement have been visible since 2011 with a coupon tracking system, new ration cards covering up to 75 per cent of rural households and widespread awareness of PDS entitlements amongst the citizens.

As noted earlier, one of the PDS commodities is kerosene oil, though the focus of much of the research on PDS has been on grain. The use of kerosene oil as a primary source of cooking and lighting has been declining, but it remains an important secondary fuel, as noted by one of the few studies carried out for investigating kerosene subsidy in India. Rao (2012) examines the kerosene subsidies in India through the tensions between the energy policy and social policy. In 2004–5 kerosene accounted for about 28 million tonnes (2 per cent) of the country's CO_2 emissions, leading to many experts suggesting replacing kerosene subsidy completely with a cleaner alternative. Rao argues that the removal of kerosene subsidy would affect approximately 800 million people who use it to supplement the main fuel, especially for lighting and cooking. Its use for lighting is dominant in the rural sector, where over 350 million people do not have access to electricity. Further, for those that do have electricity connections, the erratic supplies coupled with frequent long power outages result in high dependencies on kerosene. In addition, around 1.9 million rural households use kerosene as the primary cooking fuel.

Kerosene differs from the other PDS commodities, which can be acquired in dual markets – at the licensed FPS at subsidized prices and the other in the open market at market prices. Kerosene is sold as PDS kerosene at subsidized prices only via the FPS-licensed dealers who also sell the PDS grains. The leakage route then for kerosene is also different as there is no open market for kerosene. The leaked kerosene is instead diverted to black markets via established syndicates or local distribution channels and sold at much higher prices (Rao, 2012).

The local FPS-licensed dealer in the village scenario under discussion at the start of this chapter, over a period of four to five months, consistently put notices of 'kerosene oil not available'. The villagers were told of problems in the supplies of kerosene oil from the central government. Hushed rumours of kerosene oil being available at much higher prices than the PDS kerosene soon spread in the village. A handful of well-off villagers and poorer households desperate for some light in their dwellings during the dark winter evenings acquired the expensive kerosene. Others were pushed into deeper fuel deficits. The unavailability of the PDS kerosene and its availability in the black market caused financial hardships. This additional unplanned expenditure cut into the already fragile budgets of the mostly BPL households that comprised the village population. The village population is part of the rural demographic landscape that makes up 88.7 per cent of Bihar's total population of 103.8 million as per the Census of India, 2011.

The increasing severity of the financial burden caused by the absence of PDS kerosene and its availability at exploitative prices in the black market was picked by the village JeeVika women's SHG network. Representatives of the network sought an appointment with the district administrative officer and submitted their complaint. A speedy official inquiry into the case resulted in the cancellation of the dealer's license to run FPS and the initiation of criminal proceedings. As an interim measure, the village SHGs were given the license to sell PDS kerosene. The women organized the distribution on a couple of fixed days each month in open space as described in the introductory part of this chapter due to lack of any enclosed shop to run this operation. Apart from immediate relief to the poorer households in terms of lighting and lessening the financial burden, there were strong positive externalities of this action. The news of the dealer losing his license through the collective actions of the SHG women spread quickly in the neighbouring villages. It acted as a warning shot to FPS-licensed dealers for PDS grain and kerosene who may also have been syphoning these commodities into the open and black market. This resulted in much-improved availability and regularity for all PDS commodities.

Who are the SHG women?

JeeVika SHG network is a state-led World Bank-funded initiative launched in September 2007 in the state of Bihar. For over three decades Bihar, although rich in fertile land, continues to exhibit low HDI ranking third lowest at 0.53 in all of the twenty-three major states of India. It is India's third most populous state, with a population of 104 million, and accounts for over one-seventh of India's BPL poor. Almost 90 per cent of its population is in the rural sector with a poverty incidence at 53.5 per cent. Both health and education outcomes remain the worst in the country for the rural women in Bihar with maternal mortality at 212 (national average is 178, 2010–12) and literacy at just 53 per cent (GoI, 2016). It is characterized with rigid 'semi-feudal' tendencies, complex social-exclusion politics and FS structures. Despite agriculture being the main livelihood in the state, nearly 70 per cent of the households are landless or near landless. Twenty-five per cent of the landless belong to the lower castes, and 15 per cent are Muslim households. Mushars and Santhals are the most impoverished groups with absolute capability and asset deprivation (ADRI,[1] 2007).

In recent years, though, the progressive political leadership in Bihar has attracted support for its intensive development effort aiming to enhance social well-being and poverty reduction. The Government of Bihar (GoB), since 2005, has implemented numerous programmes to target the poorest households, build rural institutional infrastructure to encourage the poor to have bank linkages, enhance social protection and promote participatory planning. The JeeVika SHG network, also known as the Bihar Rural Livelihood Promotion Society, is a programme launched within this wider development agenda of the state. The World Bank funding enabled the establishment of an independent organization with a fully staffed setup under the state umbrella. This has the benefits of complete access to all state developmental programmes while bypassing the bureaucracy. The involvement of the World Bank team was observed to be very constructive and engaging through working closely with the JeeVika staff at the project management and implementation at the grassroots level. This included capacity building with financial support specifically at the level of banking linkages for SHGs, as well as funding for small individual projects such as a covered structure for preschool classes.

1. Asian Development Research Institute.

The conceptual model for JeeVika is located in the participatory and capability approaches to development. The building blocks of the model are 'savings-led' self-help groups comprising the poorest and the most socially excluded women. It was conceived in terms of individual institutional building situated within the discourse on well-being, empowerment, individual and community ownership and power, individual and collective capacity building, drawing on the discourse of the capability approach together with adoption of and participation in self-selected livelihoods opportunities. The focal point of the process is the individual rural woman belonging to the poorest and the most socially excluded cohort in the village. The attention to 'agency', well-being and capability expansion of these individual women underpins the JeeVika model. They address each other using the term 'didi', which in northern India is used to address an elder sister. It embodies the notion of respect and reverence given to an elder sibling within the Indian context. Drawing on a social title to formally address member colleagues of mixed-age configuration serves to instil respect and equality in participation for younger as well as older women.

Each of the ten to fifteen rural women that make up a single JeeVika SHG is the main stakeholder and the lifeline of the movement. Group members select a name for their group, which becomes the identity of the specific SHG and its members. A healthy track record of savings, lending and repayment over six months, qualifies a specific SHG to apply for bank linkages. At the same time the village SHGs are federated into a Village Organization (VO) – the next layer of the pyramid structure. There is a three-member representation from each village SHG in the VO. The membership of the VO therefore depends on the number of SHGs in the village. The VOs too have distinct identities and bank linkages. These are, in turn, federated into Community Block Organizations (CBOs). The raison d'etre for each unit of the pyramid structure – the SHG, the VO and the CBO – embedded in inclusion, participation and ownership is clearly articulated, understood and agreed by the stakeholders. The ultimate objective of the movement is to achieve better human development, self-reliance and livelihoods security. A close examination of the SHG operations reaffirms the importance of participation and unity amongst members for the collective strength of the group. Hence, the stronger the bond between the individual members, the healthier is the lifeline and the collective strength of the SHG. In addition to new bonds of collegiality and social networking created within each group, understanding of the purpose of the SHG project was clear, as the name JeeVika is translation of livelihood in Hindi. This appealed to the women to associate themselves with the SHG to improve their livelihoods and well-being.

Complexities of caste- and religion-based exclusion are engrained even *within* the lower-caste communities. The nomenclatures – JeeVika and 'didi' – appear to weaken such social rigidities and have an equalizing influence. This is further reinforced by the weekly group meetings held in rotation at the social space outside the dwellings of each member. With members seated in a circular formation on a rug provided by the host for the day, the meeting begins with a secular song in the local dialect calling for individual and collective strength, knowledge, faith and courage to follow the right path, unity in the group and community to bring happiness and well-being. This is followed by individual greetings to the group. Members first introduce themselves then greet all 'didis' with not just a 'namashkar' (hello) but 'pranam'. This again has higher connotations of respect in the cultural context, further strengthening the bond. The shy and less articulate 'didis' are encouraged with a nudge from the bold and vocal ones. The circular seating arrangement enables dispelling of any hierarchical notions that may arise out of social status or being group office bearers.

Each weekly meeting begins with re-emphasizing rules of punctuality, regular attendance or prior request for absence. In addition to meticulous minute taking, the group also maintains detailed records of the weekly savings and repayments. There are passbooks for each member as well as the group ledger. Savings and repayment are passed down the circle to each 'didi' who is encouraged to count, add their input and say it aloud, to finally reach the treasurer. The practice aims to instil a sense of ownership and entitlement amongst the SHG members by visually and physically handling their savings and repayments. A Rs.10 note growing to Rs. 150 at the end of the round certainly appeared to provide a sense of material security – the group has Rs.600 at the end of each month and the assurance of accessing this money with dignity. The implications – personal, social and economic – of the borrowing costs at 2 per cent compared with at least 10 per cent from the local moneylender are clear to the group.

The meeting agenda moves on to assess the loan applications for the group money. Each applicant makes a case outlining their need, how and by when they expect to pay and the urgency for it. The decision-making process is participatory such that all 'didis' barring the applicant discuss the proposal to arrive at a consensus. The arguments are lively both in terms of questioning the merits of the case and in supporting the application. Further, in clear contrast to a commercial lending process, the group appeared to relegate the 'ability to pay back' to a much lower priority where the need was either for life-threatening treatment or for a daughter's marriage. 'Softer' repayment terms extended over a longer period are offered to such applicants. However, concerns of accountability from the treasurer, of any defaulting repayment and savings as well as inadequate information being given indicated a strong sense of ownership of the process. 'Didis' are not wanting in vociferously expressing their views, be it a criticism of their treatment at the bank or any other village institution, concern regarding issues causing hardships or how much they wish their children to be educated so that they can live a better life than their parents. The meeting concludes with the summary of the actions to be taken and the minutes being read out aloud. And finally a 'didi' is asked to volunteer to host the next meeting in the social space near their dwellings. All go away with confirmed timing and venue for the next meeting.

The Community Mobilizer ('CM Didi'), who is a JeeVika staff and resident of the same village, facilitates bookkeeping and up-skilling of women where needed. Most members at the time of joining the SHG are illiterate using their thumb mark as signature. As part of the empowerment foci of the JeeVika SHGs, the women are encouraged to learn to sign. The sense of pride in being able to put their signature even at the age of sixty-five or more instead of the thumb mark – 'angutha chap' – for their identity is fathomless. The women maybe illiterate but they do not lack the ability to participate, comprehend, calculate, question or communicate. The wealth of knowledge and awareness reflected in both articulating and suggesting solutions to social problems such as alcoholism, poor public services delivery – in particular health services and irregularities in PDS, teacher absenteeism in the village school and lack of village roads is remarkable. It provides fertile grounds for a stimulating discourse on literacy, knowledge and understanding of their own well-being as well as that of their family. The 'didis' appear to be having an empowering experience enabling them to express their experiential knowledge, pursue the opportunities they value and live with pride and dignity.

What happened?

The unavailability of the PDS kerosene oil during the dark winter evenings when it was needed most to have even a single lantern light in the dwelling caused huge inconvenience. The majority population of the village belonged to one of the most socially and economically deprived communities, and their mud houses did not have electricity connections.

There were a few electric poles in the village and a handful of brick houses owned by the better-off villagers that were connected to the electric grid. The chronic power outages, though, rendered the electricity connection to an object of status symbol only while depending on kerosene for lighting up the house. The villagers were forced to sparingly use candles that were far more expensive than using the PDS kerosene lanterns. The licensed FPS dealer for PDS kerosene repeatedly blamed the central government supply chain for not receiving the designated quota for the village. Several neighbouring villages reported availability of PDS kerosene, albeit erratic, on some occasions.

Following a period of at least two to three weeks of acute shortage of PDS kerosene, hushed information of the availability of higher-priced kerosene at the FPS-licensed dealer spread in the village. The few well-to-do villagers were first to acquire this kerosene at more than double the price of the PDS kerosene. The poorer households who were in dire need of some lighting due to an ailing family member or children's sickness also acquired small quantities by cutting on some essentials or borrowing. Within a week while the availability of kerosene oil in the village improved, its price went up to almost three times the price of the PDS kerosene. The FPS-licensed dealer reported to having tough negotiations with some external sources to have been given small quantities of kerosene for which he had to pay. Hence, justifying the high prices he was charging.

Most villagers could not afford the costly kerosene but most ended up purchasing some amount during the four months since the PDS kerosene vanished from the FPS. Nearly all households were borrowing to meet this additional cost. As part of the weekly agenda to discuss social problems, the kerosene shortage and its availability in the black market were raised in several of the village SHGs. Many 'didis' were putting in loan applications at the weekly group meetings to seek the additional resources required to purchase the high-priced kerosene. This caused intra-group tensions on two accounts. First, the shortage was affecting everyone in the village, so why should one member have priority claim to the group savings to address the hardship over other members? The weekly savings were not sufficient to be shared between all members for each to acquire the additional money needed. Second, the primary purpose of the group savings was to enable improvement in livelihood opportunities. Loans for acquiring kerosene oil by a few members could not be justified as either facilitating livelihood or improving well-being. It was agreed to table the issue at the VO SHG meeting, which has representatives from each village SHG.

Consensus was rapidly reached at the VO SHG to go directly to the district magistrate with the complaint of severe irregularity in the PDS kerosene and its availability in the black market. The district magistrate is the administrative official who is responsible for overseeing the policy implementation and law and order in the district. The VO SHG representatives met the official and submitted a complaint. As kerosene cannot be purchased in open market, unlike other PDS commodities, its availability at higher price is a black market offence. The district magistrate made an unannounced visit to the FPS. The licensed dealer was caught red handed while dispensing kerosene in the black market. He was asked to immediately surrender the accumulated stocks of the PDS kerosene that he had been accumulating to slowly release in the black market. More importantly, his PDS kerosene license was cancelled with immediate effect. In the interim, while the process to tender for FPS license for all PDS commodities was initiated, the distribution for PDS kerosene was given to the VO SHG.

The VO SHG sought help from the office of the village head – the village Panchayat. Two men from the Panchayat office volunteered to join the VO SHG operation in distributing the PDS kerosene. It was decided to spread the distribution process over two half days each month in the open space of the village square. The day, time and venue of the distribution were communicated via the VO SHG 'didis' to their respective SHG members. The scenario captured in the beginning of this chapter describes the distribution of the PDS kerosene on one of the designated days by the VO SHG.

As noted earlier, in addition to restoring the regular availability and access to PDS kerosene for the poorer households and removing their financial burden, the VO SHG actions had positive externalities. Swift response of the administration to punish fraudulent activity sent a strong warning to all licensed PDS dealers in the neighbouring area and beyond. This resulted in improved availability and regularity of all PDS commodities throughout the region. Further, as the leakage of the PDS kerosene was exposed through the collective action of the SHGs, the JeeVika SHG women were acknowledged as an organization that could bring about change.

How did it happen?

The trigger to do something about the hardship caused by acute PDS kerosene shortages was the agency of the individual rural women – the 'didis' of JeeVika SHG. There is extensive literature on the meanings of agency, empowerment and well-being and the role these play in human development. In a very 'Sen' language Malhotra (2003, p. 3) defines agency as the ability to act on behalf of what you value and have the reason to value. Sen (1985b, p. 206) himself defines agency as 'what a person is free to do and achieve in pursuit of whatever goals or values he or she regards as important'. The 'didis' were thus exercising their individual agencies by voicing concern and expressing anger with a view to do something to change the situation. The JeeVika SHG platform offered a space where the women were 'free to do and achieve in pursuit of whatever goals', as per Sen's definition noted earlier. The action – to do something to change the situation – though, required the women to work not as a solo agent but in a group. Based on their experience of success in improving teacher absenteeism and midday meal quality in the village school, the SHG women were cognizant of the importance of collective strength.

There is rich literature on the relevance of social capital as one of the key enabling ingredients of community or collective achievements of the poor. In particular Lin (2001), Mahieu and Ballet (2001), Serageldin and Grootaert (2000) and Putnam (2000) draw attention to how the social capital of the poor enhances their bargaining power, their participation in local decision making, information sharing and social protection amongst other things. Ibrahim (2006) using these concepts and SHG case studies in Egypt has further provided an in-depth analysis of individual and collective capabilities. Ibrahim emphasizes fulfilment of self-interest and nurturing of wider communal goals as both the drivers for sustaining SHGs and expansion of capabilities through SHGs. In her later work (Ibrahim, 2008) she defines collective agency *as an exercise of human freedoms whereby a group/or a collectivity seeks to pursue goals collectively that go beyond their individual well-being concerns.* Hence, when individual goals become the goals of the community, that is, the common endeavours, the group or the community acts as a single entity. In turn, the individual agency of the members is channelled as collective agency. It is this combined effort to achieve what the group values and pooling in of social capital and other resources that constitutes collective agency.

The role of collective agency or the ability of the community to act on behalf of what the community values and has the reason to value becomes ever-more significant amidst groups experiencing both economic and social resource constraints. Individuals belonging to such deprived communities lack the confidence, literacy and information to access the opportunities and resources needed for exercising their agency to achieve their goals in life. However, pursuit of common endeavours through mechanisms such as the SHGs that deploy pooled human resources and social capital of the poor facilitates overcoming these limitations (Tiwari, 2014).

The argumentations noted earlier on collective agency as applied to the resource, poor communities in particular, capture the key narrative and group strengths of the JeeVika SHG women. They are illiterate or at best have low levels of literacy and they are resource poor. Further, while they do not necessarily lack confidence, very few, if at all any, woman on her own could mobilize community support, access her public goods entitlement or seek help from state officials. The individual goal of resisting the PDS kerosene shortage seamlessly became the goal of the SHG, as all households were adversely affected. The women's group then exercised their collective agency first by taking the issue to the VO SHG then in turn the VO SHG collectively representing the village through its delegation to the district magistrate.

The quick access to a public official by the SHG 'didis' and the swift action taken by the official to address the issue demonstrate a functioning public institutional infrastructure. Locating this within the literature on agency, Cleaver (2007, p. 226) notes the relational existence of agency, implying its use in and importance of a social context. It is this social context that shapes the opportunities and resources that can be accessed by individuals. Ibrahim and Alkire (2007) further draw attention to the opportunity structure or the institutional environment that act as prerequisites for the effective deployment of agency. This opportunity and resource structure is described as the relational agency. The SHG 'didis' thus exercised their individual agency within their specific SHG platform, which was converted to collective agency both within their SHG and in the VO SHG. They then encountered and engaged with a functioning relational agency to resolve the PDS kerosene shortage in the village and its availability in the black market. The social context created within the JeeVika SHG network enabled the women to meaningfully exert their individual and collective agencies. This facilitated the conversion of the individual goal to the community goal in addition to gaining access to complete information on the distribution of PDS commodities and the complaint process to report fraudulent activity. The SHG women deployed all three types of agencies – individual, collective and relational – to mitigate the hardship caused by the leakage of PDS kerosene.

The 'how' of the positive outcomes achieved by the 'didis' of JeeVika can also be situated and explained within the literature on the conceptions of power. Both the positive and the negative premises of the Foucauldian discourse on power are visible in the PDS kerosene episode in the village. Further, the sources of power can be traced to multiple actors in this episode – the SHGs, the FPS-licensed dealer and the government official. Insights into the multiple sources of power and beyond the territory of selected individuals or/and institutions are critical in the Foucauldian construction of the optimistic foundations of power.

A more detailed understanding of the power dynamics between the actors of the PDS kerosene case study is offered through the advancement of Luke's dimensions of power (Luke, 1974) by Gaventa (2006). In particular, the four genres of power – *within* (self-confidence and awareness of entitlements); *with* (power through finding common ground and building collective strength); *to* (opportunity to achieve and shape one's life); and lastly *over* (the traditional hierarchical power entailing domination, force, coercion and decision-making authority with a win–lose relationship) – provide a useful framework for analysing the PDS kerosene power dynamics.

The last category ('power over') was the genre exerted in the first instance by the FPS-licensed dealer over what he perceived as the powerless villagers. He exploited the villagers' need and dependency on the PDS kerosene only he could provide. In addition, he misappropriated his authority for personal gains by creating shortages and diverting the kerosene to the black market. The district magistrate also exercised the same genre of power over the PDS kerosene dealer. He used his authority vested in his official role as the guardian of law and order along with overseeing enforcement of policy. Through this institutional decision-making authority he was able to initiate a swift investigation into the complaints of the SHG women and penalize the dealer for his fraudulent activity. Further, through the same authority, the district magistrate awarded the interim dealership to the VO SHG for the distribution of PDS kerosene. It is important to note then, how 'power over' can be used for both negative and positive outcomes.

The first two genres of power – 'power within and power with' – are what the rural women acquire by becoming the 'didis' of the JeeVika SHG network. These women gain confidence by belonging to a structured network, by speaking up in the group meetings, by being able to write their signature instead of using thumb mark for identity to name. Additionally, access to group savings with dignity in case of emergency without the humiliation of borrowing from the local moneylender further boosts their confidence. An empowered 'didi' is more often than not encouraged to seek information from the Block Development Officer (BDO) regarding the numerous social protection programmes and her family's entitlements. They are able to visit the bank and talk to the bank clerks and managers about opening bank accounts, to gain information on schemes to help the poor. They are able to contact and talk to the local health worker to seek information on immunizations and their entitlements regarding the maternal health support schemes.

These rural women acquire 'power with' when some of their individual goals are converted into their particular SHG goal. It is through the group consensus for working together towards an issue that their representatives take the proposal to the VO SHG for mobilizing support of JeeVika 'didis' at the village level. Individual goals that are transitioned into community goals through this process give the collective strength to the rural women to engage with the process to bring about change and achieve the goal. The SHG women demonstrated deploying both these genres of power by first having the confidence to bring up their concern and unhappiness at the PDS kerosene shortage while being available in the black market. The desire to do something about it rapidly became the collective goal. It was the collective strength of the SHG women that powered them to escalate the matter to seek redress. The process required first and foremost knowing precisely where and how the dealer was violating regulation, what were their options to mitigate the hardship caused through the dealer's actions and what they needed to do to register a formal complaint. These features are part of the opportunity structure within the public service provision of social protection and welfare policies of a democratic state. When the women engage with this opportunity structure, they are demonstrating the 'power to' genre. This expression of power, though, entails a somewhat unspoken partnership between the state – for its functioning social policies and institutional infrastructure for justice – and the citizens to have been sufficiently empowered to connect with these offerings.

The actors in the PDS kerosene case study demonstrated deploying all four genres of power. For the resource poor women, 'power within and with' was the key driver in enabling the desired outcome. However, for them to succeed, the 'power to' in the form of a functioning public provision structure, as well as 'power over' in the form of law enforcement by the official machinery, was essential.

The interplay between agency, power and ability to bring about change can be further explained and understood within the Freireian discourse. Paulo Freire's (1970) seminal work on the dialogical encounters between individuals and the world they live in offers conceptions of how a person, however ignorant and illiterate he/she maybe, if given with proper tools, defines the world he/she lives in and also their own personal realities. The process by which individuals reflect on the problems they experience and frame their perceptions of reality in the immediate and in the larger world is known as conscientization within the Freireian discourse. Conscientization enables individuals to develop their ability to gain a critical understanding of the real world such that they are both learners and teachers to others. This helps individuals to first become aware of their agency and then understand the different ways they can exercise it in finding a solution to their problems or *changing realities of the world in which they exist.*

The JeeVika SHG platform facilitates the conscientization process such that women first discuss their experiences with societal problems and deprivations in economic and social domains in the weekly SHG meetings. This sharing of experiences amongst peers not only encourages all members to talk about their situations, but they also become aware of the range of problems that are common experience to all. An example of this is the hardship imposed on most households through the unavailability of the PDS kerosene oil and subsequently its availability in the black market. The shared experience of individual women spurred discussions in the village SHGs to collectively find a solution. The women thus first articulated the reality of their world, then reflected on their roles in engaging and addressing the problematic reality.

The convergence framework

Restoration of the PDS kerosene along with the penalty imposed on the dealer for violating regulation demonstrates achievement of the collective goal and a positive change. The pathway to this outcome, starting with the licensed dealer declaring its unavailability followed by the appearance of higher-priced kerosene in the same shop, entailed active participation of the individual, the community and the state officials. The capability approach constructions of agency and moving beyond individual to collective agency, which then engaged with the relational agency, are the core foundations of this process. However, merely having an agency is not sufficient to initiate change as a single resource poor individual alone cannot take the actions needed to address the problem. Hence, the women's individual agency would be of not much use if they were not able to mobilize group and community support to facilitate conversion of individual to collective agency. In turn, the collective agency would also not be of any use if it did not engage with the relational agency. Finally, if the relational agency representing the public provision opportunity structure, which the poor can access, does not exist or it is feeble, the efforts to engage with it would not result in the desired outcomes.

It is possible that despite the women wanting to resist and do something about the PDS kerosene shortage, they did not have the space to act and express, leading to thwarting of their individual agency. Another scenario could be meaningful exerting of individual agency at the group level but not getting sufficient support by other members. This would lead to non-conversion of individual to the group goal, hence the absence of collective agency. There can be yet another pitfall. The relational agency exists but rent-seeking behaviour and leakages are rampant within public-sector provisions, leading to a weak relational agency. Therefore, for positive change to happen, each of the three types of agencies needed to be functioning.

Within the Foucauldian discourse comprising both the negative and positive premises of power, its multiple sources of location, and further advancements of expressions of power by VeneKlasen and Miller (2002) and Gaventa (2006), the PDS kerosene episode demonstrates its amorphous existence and its necessity for change to happen. Again, while the different power genres can be both positive and negative expressions, for a positive change to happen the positive expressions of power need to reinforce and coalesce. This is essential to overcome the sum total of negative expressions of power. The powers of 'within and with' deployed by the 'didis' of JeeVika and the power 'over' exercised by the state official worked towards the same objective of restoring PDS kerosene availability. The women sought to mitigate the hardship its shortage caused to their households as their primary goal. They informed of the fraudulent activity regarding the PDS kerosene sale to the decision-making authorities. The state official, though, pursued correcting violation of regulation and addressing the problems faced by the villagers. Thus, while these two sets of actors had different outcome foci resulting from the achievement of the main objective, the attainment of the main objective itself was an end in itself. This acted as the key driver for power typologies to come together and reinforce the efforts of each actor.

These analyses of the PDS kerosene in the village in Bodh Gaya, in the state of Bihar in India, indicate that the achievements of desired outcomes are facilitated through specific configurations of agency and power facilitated by the process of conscientization. Within the agency 'lens' of the capability approach, the desired change happens when individual agency converges into collective agency and interacts with a functioning relational agency. An important caveat here is that not all individual agencies can become collective agency. This is so because each individual has different aspirations and goals for themselves and their families. Aspirations that are common and pursued by a number of individuals have the potential of becoming group and in turn community goals. Examples of individual goals that became group and community goals within the JeeVika SHG network in many villages are addressing teacher absenteeism in the village school, improving the quality of the school midday meal and restoring the PDS kerosene shortage to name a few. This confluence of the three domains of agency created conditions for the desired outcome to be achieved with a caveat that each of these domains need to be functioning. Conceptually this can be illustrated by the area A in Figure 1.

The area A represents the PDS kerosene regular distribution via the interim license to the VO SHG, the kick start of the process for recruiting new permanent licensee and the penalty imposed on the dealer selling the kerosene in the black market. In addition, the area A also captures the positive externalities of the swift action taken to curb irregularity

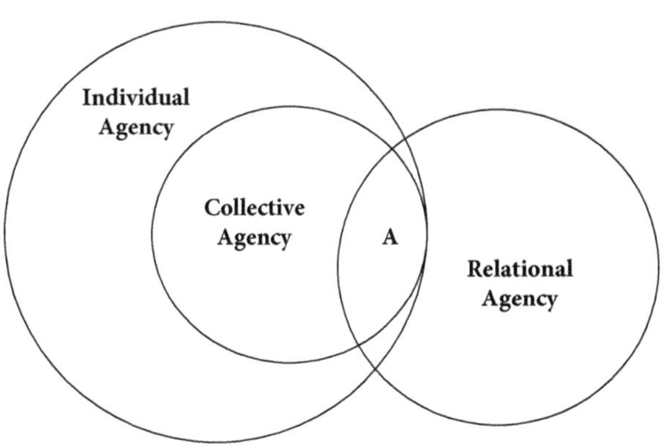

Figure 1 Conditions for achieving an outcome.

in the PDS kerosene by cancelling the dealer's license. These included improved PDS commodity supplies and its regularity in the neighbouring villages. In terms of the power analyses, the area A represents the consequences of the coming together of the 'power within', 'power with' and the positive expression of 'power to'. Within both constructs, the area A shows a configuration of convergence. As noted earlier, the SHG platform enabled consientization such that women become aware of their individual and collective agencies to then act and find a solution. Schematically then, this CF explains how the actions of the SHG women progressed and achieved the desired outcomes.

Key reflections from the 'Story So Far . . .' (Chapter 2) draw attention to the critical role of the state and its institutional capacity, partnership between the state and third sector through macro–micro linkages, grassroots engagement and ownership together with collective action as some of the factors attributed to successful interventions. A few other actors are also considered important in shaping development progress and positive change. These include Bornstein's micro actors within the emerging citizenship sector (Bornstein, 2007), political leaders and donors. These factors can be mapped to the JeeVika SHG network and to the women's actions that spurred the change in restoring PDS kerosene, as well as to the other improvements in teacher absenteeism and quality of the midday meal.

The JeeVika SHG network itself is the outcome of a close partnership between the World Bank and the GoB. As mentioned earlier, this funding allows close mentoring, monitoring and capacity building through a comprehensively staffed setup. JeeVika is a livelihood promotion project that is part of the wider progressive development agenda under the new political leadership since 2005. The institutional capacity of the state is demonstrated by the swift enforcement of regulations to restore PDS kerosene, mitigate hardship caused to the poor and penalize fraudulent activity. The partnership between the state and the grassroots third sector can be located to the communication channels and easy access to the citizens. This enabled the women's delegation to submit their grievance to the state officials. Further, the macro–micro linkages are reflected in the PDS being part of a national social protection scheme while its irregularity was identified at the micro level and addressed in partnership with the micro actors and the state. Lastly, the ownership and collective action are visible in the individual to collective agency conversion at the intra- and inter-SHG levels in the village.

The conceptual schema of the conditions needed for achieving the desired outcomes in Figure 1 broadly captures the factors highlighted earlier in the three domains of agency. Relational agency indicates the opportunity structure that can be accessed by the poor. This entails public service provision, public institutions and state bureaucracy that functions. The political will and funding, whether external or domestic, influence these factors. The individual and collective agency domains reflect ownership, collective strength and engagement with public service provision. The convergence area of the three-agency typologies shows the configuration that facilitates the outcome. This CF explains the success of PDS kerosene in the village.

The chapters that follow deploy this CF to examine and explain macro and micro progress in different contexts. The purpose is to test the CH and the validity of this conceptual tool in explaining why some interventions work.

Chapter 4

THE MACRO LANDSCAPE

DOES THE CONVERGENCE FRAMEWORK EXPLAIN DEVELOPMENT PROGRESS AT THE MACRO LEVEL?

This chapter presents analysis of development at macro level within the CF. The objective is to assess whether progress at the macro level can be explained by the CF. The selected case studies are the flagship programmes of Brazil's the Zero Hunger Programme and India's Mahatma Gandhi National Rural Employment Guarantee Act.

The CF developed in Chapter 3 offers a conceptual schema of the conditions needed for achieving the desired outcomes. Shaped by ground research along with observational and interpretive data of a case study in rural Bihar in India, the schema puts forward the CH: *a development intervention is more likely to work when there is congruence between individual goals, collective goals and the relational context.* The relational context here refers to the social-, economic- and political-policy structures. Two macro-level programmes, much acclaimed for changing the landscape of poverty in the host countries, are selected to first examine the validity of CF in explaining the success of state-led large-scale interventions and second, to test this hypothesis within macro contexts. These programmes include Brazil's Fome Zero (Zero Hunger) Programme, launched in 2003, which later became Bolsa Familia and India's National Rural Employment Guarantee Act (NREGA, 2005), which was renamed as the MGNREGS in 2009.

Fome Zero to Bolsa Familia

In 2003, soon after his presidential victory, Lula da Silva introduced the flagship project of his political career. Fome Zero was launched to fulfil his campaign pledge to eradicate hunger and ensure that every Brazilian had access to three meals a day by the end of his term. In his inauguration speech on 1 January 2003, President Lula da Silva declared:

> We are going to create appropriate conditions for all people in our country to have three decent meals a day, every day, without having to depend on donations from anybody. Brazil can no longer put up with so much inequality. We need to eradicate hunger, extreme poverty and social exclusion. Our war is not meant to kill anyone – it is meant to save lives. (Silva da et al. 2011, p. 9)

These words echoed the country's first working-class president's drive and personal commitment to addressing poverty and engaging with the chronic prevalence of inequality in Brazil. The son of sharecropping parents Luiz Ina`cio da Silva started his career as a shoe-shine boy moving up to a street vendor, a factory worker and the leader of the Metalworkers' Union in 1975. His swift launch of a campaign to protest the ruling military regime's economic policy by demanding wage increases for the workers propelled him into the national political arena. Following his arrest and release by the authorities Lula da Silva founded the Workers' Party in 1982. He stood as the party's candidate in the presidential elections thrice before being elected with a resounding mandate with over 61 per cent of the votes in 2002 (Bourne, 2008).

In 1974 the Brazilian economist Edmar Bacha used a hypothetical country 'Belindia' to describe Brazil. He used this concept to describe a country with a small wealthy population such as Belgium, surrounded by a vast impoverished population as in India. Over several decades, the richest 20 per cent in Brazil owned 58 per cent of the country's wealth while the poorest 60 per cent owned just 4 per cent (Wetzel and Econômico, 2013). Brazil along with the other countries in Latin America has experienced pervasive inequality with poverty for decades spanning over all of the twentieth century. Income inequality has been a retrograde and a stubborn feature of all of Latin America making it the most unequal region in the world (Zmerli and Castillo, 2015). This is mostly attributed to regressive distributive and social policies with non-inclusive growth despite several attempts to address it in the first half of the twentieth century (Zmerli and Castillo, 2015). Inequality in Latin America became pervasive over the years, spreading to both economic and social domains from distribution of income and assets, education and health to influence and participation as argued by Goñi, Humberto López and Servén (2011). In Brazil specifically, a high Gini Index of just under 0.6 prevailed during the 1990s. Following a healthy growth in the 1970s the country stagnated during the debt crisis of the 1980s through the early part of the 1990s. The accommodating monetary policy along with the built-up fiscal deficit resulted in hyperinflation rocketing to over 2000 per cent by 1994 (Ferreira et al. 2008). This was a period of trade distortions, chronic budget deficits, high inflation, dominance of state-run enterprises and a biased social security system that did not benefit the poor (Ravallion, 2009).

The hyperinflation was brought down to 4.7 per cent by 1997 through the country's *Real Plan* that entailed exchange rate-based stabilization and de-indexation of labour contracts. During the same period there was also a cessation of the trade liberalization process within which the quantitative restrictions and tariff fell from 56 per cent in 1988 to 14 per cent in 1994 (Kume et al., 2000). Some trade restrictions, albeit to a much lesser extent, were reintroduced under the new reforms of the Washington Consensus that included macroeconomic stability, privatization of some state-owned enterprises, fiscal discipline and trade reform. There was, however, a significant difference in how the Washington Consensus was embraced in Brazil and the other countries. Along with the policies under the Washington Consensus in Brazil a comprehensive overhauling of the social security system was undertaken (Ravallion, 2009). However, the 1999 National Household Sample Survey indicated 44 million poor people living below dollar a day who were highly vulnerable to hunger (Silva da et al., 2011, p. 19). This accounted for 2 per cent of the Brazilian population, 19 per cent of the populations of the metropolitan areas, 25 per cent of the non-metropolitan urban areas and 46 per cent of the rural population. The causes for this were attributed largely to low wages with high unemployment and underemployment amongst the poor (Silva da et al., 2011, p. 19). Further, these factors were found to spur a vicious circle of causes reinforcing hunger amongst this fragile income group. In addition to the skewed income concentration, dwindling purchasing power of a large cohort resulted in declining demand for food, preventing any expansion in the food supplies, thus leading to more unemployment. Addressing the food security problem thus required expansion of the domestic market to create jobs and boost incomes, reduce poverty and mitigate income and land inequalities as noted by Silva da et al. (2011, p. 20). These actions would remedy the situation in the mid- to long-term, though. The immediate hunger vulnerabilities of the 44 million people required direct assistance.

What is Fome Zero? and What is Bolsa Familia?

The Fome Zero project in Brazil is underpinned by the country's undisputed track record in social policy foci through its comprehensive social safety nets since the 1980s (Hall, 2006). While it was weakened during the deregulation paradigm of the Washington Consensus, Brazil stands out for the continuation and expansion of its social protection infrastructure during this period as noted earlier.The tools deployed for strengthening social protection, though, have been severely contested for feeble distributional impacts in a way that the higher income groups became the main beneficiaries of the subsidies in the domains of health, education and pensions.

The policy foundations of Fome Zero were built on insights from the Federation Constitution of 1988 that included new social rights; Food Security Council, 1993 and the National Conference on Food Security in 1994. Additionally, the awareness of the food security problem at the national level and the social mobilization around the issue was galvanized by the 'Citizens' Action against Hunger and Poverty for Life' campaign soon after. The campaign also revived Josue` de Castro's 1946 'Geography of Hunger' discourse (Silva da et al. 2011), thus drawing in the richness of the literary and cultural memories. The Zero Hunger Project was conceived as the blueprint for the food security policy in Brazil by the Citizenship Institute in 2001. The head of the institute at the time was Luiz Ina`cio Lula da Silva, also the Workers' Party candidate for the forthcoming national elections. The Zero Hunger Project became the key strategy for carving out the national economic and social policy arena soon after Lula's presidential victory.

The bedrock of the Fome Zero was the belief that the right to food is a key constituent of all other rights – civil, social, economic, political and cultural. The driver for this was the conviction that all citizens should have access to sufficient food to meet their nutritional requirements with dignity. Further, for a society to be called civilized, the nation needs to ensure food and nutritional security to all. Another key pillar of the Fome Zero narrative was the mobilization of citizens and their participation at all levels was considered essential for its progress (Silva da et al. 2011). Given that the main cause of hunger was access to food rather than insufficient availability of food as pointed earlier, resolving the hunger problem required addressing food security. In addition to combining economic and social policy focus to seek complementarity in mitigating income and non-income poverties, Fome Zero also included a range of emergency strategies. These were geared to supporting families already facing hunger and living in high levels of deprivations.

The Fome Zero project comprised a three pronged policy foci that included structural policies, specific policies and local policies (Aranha, 2011, p. 88). *The structural policies* engaged with the macroeconomic root causes of fragile food security, tackling employment, education and healthcare, agrarian reform and food distribution policies. *The specific policies* focused on immediate action packages directed at families experiencing multiple hardships and hunger. These included direct cash transfer, food distribution and food quality policies. The *local policies* tackled grassroots mobilization to promote food and nutritional security through a range of measures and provide technical assistance to small farmers. These three policy domains were implemented through four specific programmes: Expanded Access to Food, Strengthening Family Farming, Promotion of Productive Inclusion and Mobilization Processes.

Fome Zero was also considered an umbrella project that brought together several existing conditional cash transfer (CCT) initiatives before adding some new programmes. The theoretical underpinning of the CCTs is that investment in a social contract between the beneficiary families and the state would lead to improvement and expansion of human capital. The investment is in the form of direct cash transfers to the beneficiary families in return for fulfilling conditions such as school attendance and regular visits to health clinics (Rawlings, 2004; Hanlon et al. 2010). The existing CCTs included *Bolsa Escola* for improving school attendance, *Bolsa Alimentacao* for improving maternal nutrition, *PETI* programme to address child labour and *Auxilio Gas* for subsidized cooking gas. A new initiative of credit-card-based food entitlement *Carto Alimentacao* was added (Hall, 2006).

Within six months of the launch of the Fome Zero in early 2003 with much hope and zeal amongst the public and the policymakers, several operational challenges surfaced. These included feeble integration and complementarity between its different programmes, excessive levels of centralization, high administrative and implementation costs and targeting errors of up to 30 per cent (Hall, 2006). To address these problems and also to turn the growing disillusionment of the public, all CCTs were grouped under the new banner of Bolsa Familia. The new structure not only reconciled the administrative costs with overall reductions, but it also injected new synergies through targeting household units across all its programmes. The scheme targeted the very poor with household incomes up to $23 per month and poor with household incomes between $23.5 and $46 per month. Bolsa Familia thus consolidated all CCTs and remained under the wider umbrella of Fome Zero.

A distinct feature of both the wider Fome Zero programme and the Bolsa Familia was the robust endorsement the programmes received from international donors such as the IMF, the World Bank and the Inter-American Development Bank. This resulted in funding flows of just over US$2.5 billion, which amounted to a quarter of the total Bolsa Familia outlay. The scale of Bolsa Familia in terms of its reach and budget suggests its focus on poverty reduction beyond the original objectives of food and nutritional security (Chmielewska and Souza, 2011, p. 5).

How did it work?

The key principles that have largely shaped the complex implementation framework of the Fome Zero are, first, hunger is a manifestation of multidimensional poverty, with deprivations in incomes, health, education and participation to name a few. Second, food and nutritional security is a human right of every citizen. And, third, mobilization of citizens and communities together with their participation at all levels is essential for the progress of Fome Zero. These principles have been the driver for the emphasis on combining structural changes and short-term actions together with its multi-sectoral intervention approach. This was implemented, as noted earlier, through the three domains of *structural*, *specific* and *local* polices embodied in four wide sectors of *Access to Food*, *Family Agriculture*, *Income generation* and *social mobilization*, as noted earlier. The primary focus of the structural and the specific policy domains covered a comprehensive range of interventions. These entailed integrated social and economic actions, in addition to the emergency support where needed. Hence, the agricultural reform comprised the national plan together with emergency settlement plan for 60,000 families living in camps as well as pulling out 40,000 families living in precarious settlements. The programme against illiteracy entailed pre-literacy courses in municipalities covered by the Fome Zero as well as educational programme on agricultural reform targeted at the youth and adults (Takagi, 2011).

The multi-sectoral approach of Fome Zero was directed at the federal level as well as within its 26 states and 5,564 municipalities. At the federal level institutional expansion through new ministry was created to oversee the coordination of a number of existing policies that were to be implemented by different ministries. The ministry was also responsible for new policies that had not been adopted earlier. These included both macro- and micro-level engagement through food card programme, food and nutrition education, food security stocks, support for marketing family farm produce, incentives for agriculture and agroindustry, support for local initiatives such as setting up subsidized restaurants for people on low incomes, food banks, food procurement schemes for hospitals, day-care centres and schools (Takagi, 2011, p. 58). Thus, a top-down framework was firmly moored into the grassroots initiatives. Further, in addition to addressing access and affordability constraints, the project also paid attention to awareness raising, offering information and knowledge regarding the value of nutrition and food amidst the poorer cohort.

In addition to situating hunger and food security in a multidimensional deprivation context, requiring a multi-pronged intervention, participatory mechanisms were integral to the Fome Zero strategy. This was demonstrated at the embryonic stage of the project in 2003, with the re-establishment of National Food and Nutritional Safety Council (CONSEA). The CONSEA was a consultative instrument that brought together the civil society and the government through national conferences and workshops. It functioned through creating twenty-seven state-level councils and numerous municipality-level councils.

A novel approach of decentralizing implementation, monitoring and local initiatives was carried out through the creation of a multitude of locally elected Managing Committees (MCs) at the municipality level. The MCs were given capacity-building input by the municipalities in a range of skills and entrusted with the tasks of selection of the poorest families to include as beneficiaries, track the nutritional status of the beneficiary families, monitor all other programmes within Fome Zero being implemented in the municipality and building of water reservoirs where needed.

This approach was given a fillip by the widespread use of different modes of media at the local and national levels to communicate to the common people the purpose and functioning of MCs and about the 'fight against hunger' Fome Zero programme. Amidst growing positive public opinion, the MC expansion spread swiftly within the municipalities. The MCs enabled the local communities to be aware of the families being assisted by the Fome Zero and allowed them to engage with the process. This was a huge contrast to poor transparency in the selection and benefit process within social protection targeting in the previous decades. The direct involvement of the communities in MCs immensely empowered the civil society (Takagi, 2011, p. 66), further boosting their participation. The MC network rapidly became the key operational line of Fome Zero.

Another defining feature of Fome Zero was the official acceptance of voluntary participation in both cash and kind. This made it distinct to other state-run social protection programmes in Brazil and elsewhere in other developing countries. This was again innovative in fully harnessing the goodwill and energy of the volunteers through a formal channel in the programme with clearly defined objectives. These included creating mechanisms to ensure participation of the civil society, establishing campaigns for donations of food and cash and seeking joint accountability of ministries involved in Fome Zero (Takagi, 2011, p. 82). These actions led to setting up of systems to collect food donations and its quick dispensation to the beneficiaries with the help of an electronic database monitored in real time. A toll-free hotline for the Fome Zero project was established in 2003. Further, within first twelve months of its launch, close to a hundred non-state organizations had become part of Fome Zero on the basis of their social inclusion initiatives. Also, as part of facilitating volunteering activities for Fome Zero, over 1,400 organizations were allowed to display the Fome Zero logo in public spaces and events to collect funds. Much of these were deployed to building reservoirs in the dry regions of the country.

The attempts to incorporate non-state actors in Fome Zero extended beyond civil society participation at the grassroots to Corporate Social Responsibility (CSR) and key role of NGOs in delivering programmes across different sectors. Companies were encouraged to direct their CSR initiatives to food security activities, which led to the formation of the Apoio Femo Zero (AFZ, Zero Hunger Support Association). Over the years the AFZ has gained much recognition for running school meal projects, water storage provisions and capacity building for civil society. Numerous NGOs have been working alongside state actors in all the three policy domains. Examples of this complementary relationship are seen in the micro-credit agencies working with the official banks to deliver solidarity-based credit schemes. These are offered to finance, production and marketing of family farmers. Additionally, NGOs join in the government in the Workers' Food Programme, food security for mother and child programmes, running of day-care centres, administering food- and nutrition-related educational programmes to name a few (Belik, 2011).

What has it achieved?

Bolsa Familia is the major component of the Fome Zero programme. As noted earlier, this cash transfer programme is based on conditions of familial behaviour ensuring school attendance and health clinic visits for children. It is considered one of the largest CCT programmes in the world reaching to 99.7 per cent of the country's municipalities. After a decade of its launch in 2003, it covers 13.8 million families or just under 50 million people that make up 26 per cent of Brazil's population (Pereira, 2015).

Within the limitations and challenges to policy impact analysis in terms of data requirements (Chmielewska and Souza, 2011, p. 30), the key achievements of Fome Zero are highly noteworthy. Brazil's historic high-income concentrations showed a declining trend for the first time in decades. The Gini coefficient fell from 0.594 to 0.544 between 2001 and 2008 (Chmielewska and Souza, 2011, p. 30). Bolsa Familia's biggest success was in reaching the most deprived families that had tenaciously remained outside of the previous social safety net programmes. The targeting mechanisms of Bolsa Familia are acknowledged by the World Bank as being amongst the most effective in reaching the poorest (World Bank, 2015). While smaller in its financial outlay of just 0.5 per cent of the GDP when compared with Brazil's Social Security programmes that amount to over 10 per cent of the country's GDP (OECD, 2014, p. 3), 94 per cent of Bolsa Familia's funds reach the poorest 40 per cent. This resulted in notable improvements across multiple domains including education, health, employment, food security and housing. Underweight children in the under five years category declined from 4.2 per cent to 2.0 per cent by 2014 (UNICEF, 2016). Poor households facing food insecurity declined from 34.9 per cent to 30.2 per cent in five years between 2004 and 2009 (Chmielewska and Souza, 2011, p. 30). Additionally, the proportion of population living below $1.25 fell from 25.6 per cent in 1990 to 4.8 per cent in 2008 (Chmielewska and Souza, 2011, p. 30). Further, under 5 mortality in Brazil fell from 61 deaths per 1,000 live births in 1990 to 16 by 2015. The opportunities for children to be enrolled and complete schooling through financial support increased the chance of fifteen-year-old girls by 21 per cent (World Bank, 2015). Brazil met all the targets of the MDG 1 in 2015.

In addition to reaching the most vulnerable families and bringing down the overall poverty, Fome Zero, and Bolsa Familia in particular, has been able to arrest intergenerational poverty. This was made possible by enabling the poorest households to access social and economic opportunities.

The pitfalls

The challenges faced by Fome Zero can be grouped into two categories. The first can be located into the principle of conditionality that underpins the CCTs. The second set of problems can be situated in the design and implementation of the CCT tool. The theoretical basis for *conditionality* in cash transfers is that one of the ways human circumstances and opportunities in life can be enhanced is by participating in a social contract. This social contract entails direct cash transfers to families in return for ensuring children's school attendance and regular visits to health clinics. The rationale is that by focusing on children, the progressive improvements in their education and health would expand life opportunities and break the transmission of intergenerational poverty.

The imposition of the conditionality criterion poses two challenges. First, violations of social obligations of regular screening and vaccinations for children as well as school attendance are problematic to monitor. This is so, as teachers and health practitioners are often unwilling to report irregularities (Hall, 2006, p. 703). Additionally, local officials and municipalities are easily influenced by the elites who can skew the beneficiary selection process, further reinforcing a culture of clientelism. The grassroots organizations who were envisaged as the independent monitors are often too closely aligned with political parties. Second, the increasing dependence on state handouts to support livelihoods is critiqued for dampening incentives for people to become more self-reliant (Hall, 2006, p. 703). Sometimes referring to it as the beggar's grant. However, Watts (2013) argues that the beneficiaries of Bolsa Familia are poor because of lack of opportunities or inability to access the opportunities and not because they don't want to or don't know how to work. This rationale has been corroborated largely by the progress made by the recipients of the programme.

The biggest hurdle in the implementation of Fome Zero programmes is reported to be the politicization of the project and its use as a vote-catching mechanism. The ruling party as well as the opposition ground their claim to be more pro-poor based on either the current reach of the CCTs or its proposed modified version. The social focus is often hijacked by political messages and propaganda. Additionally, populist handouts, high taxes and poor public service delivery further reinforce public fatigue towards false promises made by the politicians, as argued by Barnes (2013). Another impediment in the design of Fome Zero is the scope for resource leakages, fraud and misuse of the targeting system to favour the wealthier populations. Thus, with access to the appropriate political networks, under reporting of incomes, non-compliance of conditionalities and absence of local municipalities was overlooked. Hall (2006) further indicates local connections and contact in the mayoral offices played a crucial role in the beneficiary selection process.

Fome Zero and the convergence framework

The CF, developed in Chapter 3, explored the key conceptual schema of conditions needed for achieving the desired outcomes. The schema put forward the CH: *a development intervention is more likely to work when there is congruence between individual goals, collective goals and the relational context.* The analysis in this section examines the tangible progress in addressing food security, housing, children's health and education and in reaching the most deprived families attributed to Fome Zero within CF. The objective is to assess whether the CH holds in the context of Fome Zero in Brazil.

As pointed earlier, the bedrock of the Fome Zero was the belief at the individual and societal levels that the right to food is a key constituent of all other rights – civil, social, economic, political and cultural. Thus, there was a strong individual and collective agency that aspired to overcome the various dimensions of social and economic poverties that pose challenges to achieving food security. The driver for this was the conviction that all citizens should have access to sufficient food to meet their nutritional requirements with dignity. Further, for a society to be called civilized, the nation needs to ensure food and nutritional security to all, thus suggesting that the state has a role (the relational agency) in enabling the food security of every citizen. Another key pillar of the Fome Zero narrative was the mobilization of citizens, and their participation at all levels was considered essential for its progress (2006). This further emphasized the importance of collective agency.

The overall structure of Fome Zero was therefore firmly grounded in facilitating the congruence of relational, collective and the individual agency. The state-led relational agency created a robust mechanism that offered opportunities in domains that affected the most deprived communities while at the same time facilitating the direct participation of these communities to access the opportunity infrastructure. This approach resulted in reaching the poorest families who had been perpetually left out of the social safety net programmes. Thus, while driven by a strong relational agency, Fome Zero ensured individual and community voices to be included in the needs' identification, selection, engagement and implementation processes. The participatory mechanisms were made integral to all the Fome Zero projects at both the micro and the macro levels as demonstrated by its consultative instrument CONSEA. This created a platform for dialogue and exchange of ideas between the civil society and the government in real time, which worked through a network of state-level councils and numerous municipality-level councils. The networks were further strengthened by delegating the creation and support of local initiatives, implementation and monitoring to a multitude of locally elected MCs, thus using a strong relational agency to empower and facilitate the convergence of the individual and the collective agencies.

Fome Zero's approach of embracing the multidimensionality of deprivation experienced by the poorest families led to a multi-forked intervention strategy. This strategy helped informational campaigns on health, nutrition and upskilling of the poorest who had remained outside of the social safety net. These actions in turn further encouraged a wider engagement and buy-in into the Fome Zero schemes from the most deprived people. In this way, the Fome Zero strategy added yet another pathway that reinforced the concurrence of common goals of the individual, the community and the state. The efforts were acclaimed (World Bank, 2015) for engaging the most multidimensionally impoverished families resulting in notable improvements across multiple domains including education, health, employment, food security and housing. Brazil met all the targets of the MDG 1 in 2015.

Table 1 highlights complementarity and the convergence of the state-led relational agency with that of the community and the individual. Fome Zero created a relational agency that not only offered an opportunity infrastructure to address the impoverishments of the poorest but also empowered the citizens both as individuals and as community to exercise their agency and participate in decisions that affected their life. As an example, the relational agency offered awareness campaigns and support on health, nutrition, literacy targeted to the poorest people, the community and the non-state actors. This galvanized the exercise of agency through direct participation in the schemes and putting forward individual initiatives to address food

Table 1 Fome Zero and Agency/Goals

Individual	Community/collective	State/relational
Awareness of Right to food – key constituent of civil, social, economic, political and cultural rights	All citizens should have access to sufficient food to meet their nutritional requirements with dignity	In a civilized society, the nation needs to ensure food and nutritional security to all
High individual participation in all Fome Zero schemes	Mobilization of citizens and community participation at all levels	State infrastructure and opportunities to facilitate access to education, livelihoods and healthcare
Micro initiatives of subsidized restaurants for low-income people, food banks, food procurement for hospitals, day-care centres and schools	Engagement of non-state actors – NGOs and private sector – to support food security activities, water storage provisions, capacity building	State-led awareness campaigns on health, nutrition, literacy. Formation of country-wide MC network to enable grassroots participation

Source: Author's research.

security in the community, in the hospitals and in the schools. At the same time, several community-led and private sector actors join to deliver the Fome Zero schemes, to complement the schemes through initiatives that address local needs and to connect the communities with the opportunity structure.

The fault lines of Fome Zero discussed earlier in the chapter indicate a weakened relational agency resulting from a wide range of events that in turn enfeebled the opportunity structure and the empowerment mechanisms to engage the poor. These events included irregularities and violations in implementation going unreported and other processes being skewed in favour of the elite. The culture of clientelism further politicized Fome Zero as a vote-catching mechanism. Other impediments to a strong functioning relational agency included resource leakages, fraud, non-compliance of conditionalities and absence of local municipalities in the second phase of the Fome Zero. The first phase of Fome Zero and its various schemes saw a strong convergence between the objectives of the state-run Fome Zero project and those of the individuals and communities in addressing hunger, poor health, illiteracy and overall improvement in the lives of the poor. The outcomes in terms of addressing hunger and lifting people out of poverty are applauded globally (Graziano da Silva, 2019). The pitfalls outlined earlier eroded some of its effectiveness, though the Fome

Zero model has been adopted in several countries in Asia and Africa with Malabo Declaration, to end hunger in Africa 2025. Additionally, the political-will-driven Fome Zero model has been instrumental in shaping the global goal of achieving Zero Hunger by 2030 (SDG 2).

Mahatma Gandhi National Rural Employment Guarantee Act (2009)

The post-independence policy focus in India was to lift the country out of the de-industrialsation trajectory that resulted from the colonial policies designed to benefit Britain. The decline of traditional industries led to millions of Indians losing their livelihood (Chaudhuri, 1998) and an impoverished India becoming a supplier of raw to the industrial expansion in Briton. The handful of modern industries that sprung up were too few and far from absorbing the vast pool of indigenous labour skilled in traditional industry. Planning Commission, the body entrusted to spur economic growth and development in India, was created in 1950. Within a mixed economy approach, while the public sector was to be the driver for the key sectors, the private sector was to operate within a regulated framework to ensure compliance with the national plans. The focus of this economic growth model was on industrial expansion through investment in the capital goods sector or the heavy industries. It was envisaged that this expansion would lead to higher industrial output and income in the long run. Much to the chagrin of the proponents of the architects of India's growth plan, despite achievements in creating an industrial base and above moderate growth, high poverty levels and unequal opportunities for the masses remained tenacious several decades into post-independence era.

Rural poverty reduction in particular has been a central concern of the Indian policymakers since the country's independence over seventy years back in 1947. The first census in Independent India conducted in 1951 showed a population of 360 million, with 18 per cent literacy and a life expectancy of thirty-two years. Over 82 per cent of this population lived in rural India in 1951. Fast-forward to the turn of the century, while progress was made during these five decades, India's performance in poverty reduction was at best sluggish with a burgeoning 743 million rural population, which accounted for 72 per cent of the total population and a literacy of 58 per cent. Ravallion's (2009) comparative study of poverty reduction in India, China and Brazil indicates a head count ratio of 42 per cent in India in 2005 with over three-fourths of the poor living in rural India. Thus, around 300 million rural people lived below the poverty line. The study further shows the steep decline in the headcount ratio in China during the same period to 16 per cent in 2005, having started just at a marginally better position than India in 1981.

Cognizant of the persistent nature of rural poverty and its magnitude, Government of India has implemented various rural development, social protection and agricultural schemes. These include the launch of Green Revolution in 1965, Integrated Rural Development Programme in 1978, Pradhan Mantri Gramin Awas Yojana in 1985 and Jawar Gram Samridhi Yojana in 1999. These and several other rural development targeted programmes did not yield the expected outcomes (Dikshit and Sharma, 2017) with only marginal changes in the rural poverty levels as also noted by Ravallion (2009). Further, domains of disadvantage more specific to rural context comprised caste such that 80 per cent of rural poor came from lower castes, land ownership with over 20 million landless households and millions with insecure rights to land ownership (IFAD, 2019), gender and employment. Some of the factors that led to the unsatisfactory performance of these programmes were located in poor coordination, planning and timely resourcing (Dikshit and Sharma, 2017). The slow progress in mitigating rural poverty and recognition of the problems noted earlier led to a critique of these efforts and rethink of the policy focus. The government introduced a new act building on its long history of social protection initiatives but extending it to also cover the unemployed and disadvantaged groups in rural India (Ehmke, 2016). This act was called the National Rural Guarantee Act 2005 (NREGA) and launched in the Parliament on 7 September 2005. It was implemented in three phases between 2006 and 2008 covering almost 600 districts in the country.

What is MGNREGA?

In 2009, NREGA was renamed MGNREGA, though its theoretical foundations, rationale and focus remained the same as NREGA. A key distinguishing feature between the previous rural employment/social protection schemes and MGNREGA is its legislative stature giving it a legal standing as an Act of the Parliament. Three theoretical constructs that have shaped the MGNREGA policy framework to further the social protection agenda of the government include the rights-based entitlement approach, demand-based employment and citizen-centred monitoring. Thus, while MGNREG Act was new, it was grounded in the historical legacy of India's efforts into social protection for the marginalized communities since her independence in 1947. A multitude of schemes designed to help the rural poor have also been integral to the country development plans since the beginning in the 1950s (Ehmke, 2012).

Breitkreuz et al. (2017) cluster the key objectives of the MGNREG Act into the following four domains: social protection; guaranteed wage labour opportunities for the marginalized and the most disadvantaged groups including women and the lower castes; rural livelihood security and democratic engagement to achieve inclusive growth; building and strengthening rural infrastructure through irrigation and water security, soil conservation and improved land productivity. The bedrock of the MGNREG Act is the entitlement of 100 days of paid work at the statutory minimum wage to an adult member of every rural household. This employment guarantee is for unskilled manual work with the insurance that if the job is not offered within fifteen days of the application being made, the state would pay unemployment allowance (Breitkreuz et al., 2017). The specific employment itself is grounded in a bottom-up planning mechanism involving the grassroots community to identify and prioritize the infrastructure needs of the village. Other core features of the MGNREG Act include the legally binding universal access to all rural households; projects based on unskilled work are prioritized, irrespective of the skills level to further widen participation; these projects are to be situated within 5 kilometres of the village to facilitate access to all; a third of the total participant pool was reserved for women and preference given to the lower castes (Ehmke, 2016).

The employment entitlement of MGNREG Act is rooted in the assumptions of participants' knowledge of their rights, access to public provisions within the Act and ability to claim their entitlement (Ehmke, 2016). Cognizant of the multiple deprivations experienced by the intended participants, the MGNREG Act has inbuilt campaigns for education and information dissemination that are mandatory. The respect for the rights and dignity of the people is considered paramount in the MGNREG Act. This is facilitated through a participatory mechanism in deciding the selection of public works for their village. Further, the act has legislative provision for the redressal of grievance of the participants and villagers.

How does it work?

The three foundational pillars of MGNREGA, namely rights-based entitlement and demand-driven employment; citizens' rights in planning and monitoring and universal access to all rural households each have distinct mechanisms of implementation. Within the overarching aim of providing 100 days of employment accompanied with empowerment, civic participation and financial inclusion of women, village-level governance and decision making are considered paramount. Thus, the final word on the selection of work and its implementation are delegated to the local village-level elected bodies (Gram Panchayats, GP) of the Panchayat Raj Institutions (PRI).

The GPs are considered the linchpin of the bottom-up processes that were conceptualized to deliver the MGNREGA. These locally elected bodies are represented by the village assembly (Gram Sabha). The key task of the village assemblies is to carry out a scoping of the possible works needed in the village and forward to the local authorities for technical clearance. As per the MGNREGA, 50 per cent of the authorized works should come from the pool proposed by the village assemblies. The other critical function of the village assembly is to administer social audits bi-annually. The process entails allowing public access to all MGNREGA documentation regarding approved works, job cards, wage slips, funds received and the policy files for scrutiny at the village meetings. The process, in addition, encourages individual and collective complaints to uncover irregularities, fraud and misappropriation of funds at the district level. Clear guidelines and mechanisms are outlined to take forward the complaints and the grievance redressal process. To further reinforce the dispensation of justice at the GP level, there is also the provision of an independent body at the district level. This body can be approached by individuals as well as groups to register a complaint on any dimension of the MGNREGA remit (Ehmke, 2016).

The three pillars of the MGNREGA framework noted earlier – rights-based entitlement and demand-driven employment, citizens' rights in planning and monitoring, and universal access to all rural households – can only be exercised and function effectively if the rural citizens are aware of their rights and the provisions within MGNREGA. The MGNREGA includes central government co-funded Information and Education Campaigns with pictographic display of all the information and activities.

The recipient actions entail two key steps. The first step on the part of the beneficiaries is to get the Job Card either an individual one or the family card which has all the personal and demographic details to avoid misuse. The same card is used to record the number of days worked. The second step is to find an employment in public works for oneself through an official application submitted to the MGNREGA, though this was relaxed to informal and oral applications to widen the access.

While the MGNREGA offers universal access, it recognizes the potential for the most vulnerable groups to be left out through somewhat a 'crowding out' effect as the well-to-do in the village are quick to avail these opportunities. Thus, the Act lays out special provisions and ring-fenced allocations for lower castes, persons with disability and women. With rural female work force participation of just 38 per cent compared with 84 per cent for men in 2011, as per the National Sample Survey Office (NSSO, 2013), the Act stipulates equal wages with men, one-third of works reserved for women, childcare facilities on site and the works to be near the women's home.

The MGNREGA wages were originally set in line with the National Minimum Wage Act but have been revised to higher levels. However, these remain lower than the minimum wages in several states, as noted by Shah et al. (2012). The central government has subsequently accepted pegging the wages to the Consumer Price Index with 2009 as the baseline. Other safeguard mechanisms in the MGNREGA include provision for timely payments through banks and post offices, cash benefits or the unemployment allowance to those individuals who were given employment within fifteen days of making the application, the permissible works to prioritize infrastructure that is pro-poor and labour protection schemes that offer onsite first aid, safe water drinking, childcare and injury insurance (Ehmke, 2016).

What has it achieved?

The MGNREG Act is attributed to significantly further India's social protection reach by offering income security to millions of her rural citizens since its inception in 2006 (ILO, 2014). On an average 50 million rural households were provided employment at the time of the 2011 census. This also indicated the expansion of employment in MGNREG-supported public works by eight times the level in 2006 (GoI, 2013). The Government of India report (GoI, 2013) further acknowledged the upward push on rural wages and its consequences on declining rural poverty trends to be one of the largest amongst the country's numerous social protection schemes.

Another landmark achievement of the MGNREG Act has been in the domain of rural female work participation rates. Female participation rose 10 per cent in the first couple of years from a dismal 38 per cent at the launch of the MGNREG Act in 2009. The MGNREG Act has further encouraged women to seek work by offering higher wages at par with those offered to men as well as being seen as respectable work. The notion of respectability linked with the MGNREG-supported work is situated in the perception of the state being a safe and trustworthy agency and the confidence therein that these works are socially acceptable, as also noted by Khera and Nayak (2009). Additionally, the paid work opportunities are reported to have empowered women in making economic and social choices in life in some states.

Rural infrastructure and asset creation, where built as per the needs of the poor and sustainably used, is also considered a tangible benefit of the MGNREG public works provision. On a positive note, Ehmke (2016), and Dikshit and Sharma (2017) amongst others point to the potential of the MGNREG Act in transforming the lives of the rural poor in both economic and social domains. In particular, if the model is implemented as laid out in the Act, it is shown to have empowered the marginalized, reduce dependence and exploitative relationship with money lenders as well as offer local employment opportunities.

The pitfalls

There is comprehensive literature that evaluates the full minutiae of the MGNREG Act. While most studies acknowledge its innovative and inclusive framework, the underlying assumptions, implementation, practice and outcomes have attracted much critique. The CAG Report (2013) indicated fundamental gaps in the actualization of the MGNREG Act. The village assemblies (Gram Sabhas), considered the key unit and drivers of the citizen-centred planning in multitude of regions, either did not exist, existed but did not take place regularly or were outposts for a few vested interests in the village. This in turn made the village assembly anything but a people's representative forum and resulted in the work selection process favouring the rich and the powerful in the village. Another fallout of the privileged membership of the Gram Sabha was the indifference of the villagers to MGNREGA activities leading to their poor engagement in the selection or the social audit process.

The rights-based entitlement to work and demand for other social provisions within the MGNREG Act assumed a rural person's knowledge of the Act and where needed the information gap to be filled by the central government co-funded Information and Education Campaigns (IEG). Bahuguna, Pandey and Soodan (2016), in their study of the socio-economic impact of MGNREGA in the state of Uttra Khand, found lack of awareness of the schemes, rights and provisions within the MGNREG Act as the single most impediment to the implementation of MGNREGA. This insight is further corroborated by the CAG Report (CAG, 2013), which found that in one-third of the places inspected IEGs had never taken place. Further, there was wide variation in the progress between the different states such that IEC plans did not exist in twelve states with another five states showing large underspend in the IEC funds.

A number of studies at the state-level indicate a plethora of failings in several key policy domains of the MGNREG Act after running for almost a decade. Agarwal (2016) highlights the week enforcement of the MGNREG Act specifically within the core areas of providing employment, delays in wage payments and violations in entitlements. This study shows the overall declining trend in employment generation with some states falling behind by up to 60 per cent in years eight and nine. In other states, the volume of work was as little as just five days in the entire year. The MGNREGA commitment to pay wages within fifteen days after the completion of work was found to have been floundering in meeting this obligation with up to 70 per cent overall of MGNREGA work payments being late in the country.

Several stipulations and safeguards within MGNREG Act intended as measures of protection and inclusivity have subsequently been watered down. Thus, the MGNREGA wages are delinked from the National Wage Act and instead fixed by the central government as pointed by Dreze (2015). This has resulted in MGNREGA wages being lower than the minimum wage in several states. Further, the compensation for late payments has been fixed at a much lower rate than the original stipulation, and the ring-fenced quota of 3 per cent allocation for persons with disabilities has been withdrawn. Another safeguard mechanism removed at the end of ten years is the unemployment allowance to those unable to secure work under MGNREGA. Additionally, the worksite facilities aimed at facilitating women's work participation in particular are scarce or not functioning. Perhaps the most disappointing shift has been with regards to the budget restrictions and release of funds by the central government together with the near collapse of the grievance redressal mechanism.

Despite initial rejection of the MGNREG Act by the new BJP-led government in 2014, the Act has not been withdrawn and has in fact received new funds and incentives for improvements. Further, MNREGA's closely embedded structure in the rural communities enabled the critical livelihood support and food provision in large parts of rural India during the first four months of the pandemic since the end of March 2020.

MGNREGA and the convergence framework

The CF, developed in Chapter 3, explored the key conceptual schema of conditions needed for achieving the desired outcomes. The schema put forward the CH: *a development intervention is more likely to work when there is congruence between individual goals, collective goals and the relational context*. The analysis in this section examines the tangible progress in social protection, guaranteed wage labour opportunities for the marginalized and rural livelihood security attributed to MGNREG Act within CF. The objective is to assess whether the CH holds in the context of the MGNREG Act in India.

Given that NREG Act (2005), which became the MGNREG Act in 2009, emerged as a direct policy response to the country's persistent nature of rural poverty and its magnitude, it can be said that the Act was state-led relational-agency driven and that relational agency itself was robust. As noted in Chapter 3, relational agency is the opportunity and resource structure located within the public policy and institutional infrastructure. The relational agency in the context of MGNREGA builds on the country's long history of social protection as pointed out earlier in this chapter. The key actor in the relational agency for MGNREGA is then the central government, that is, the GoI. Other important stakeholders that play a crucial role in the MGNREGA relational agency include the state-level institutional infrastructure agents – the Ministry of Rural Development – the district-level policymakers' and the PRI at the village level (Gram Sabha or the village assembly) who are responsible for the implementation of the MGNREG Act.

The other two components of the CF are the collective agency and the individual agency as noted in Chapter 3. The collective agency in the MGNREGA context can be said to be represented by both the members of the village assembly and the elected office-holders of the village assembly who head the Panchayats in each village. All villagers are lawful members of the village assembly and invited and encouraged to participate in MGNREGA matters. Members participating in village assemblies that discuss the MGNREGA work priorities for the village or the grievance redressal process therefore collectively act as one voice pursuing a common goal. The elected office bearers are given the mandate collectively by the villagers to represent them in all MGNREGA matters that concern the village. Each adult individual who is resident of the village with interest in MGNREGA, albeit not all the same, constitutes the single units that represent the individual agency.

The modus operandi of the MGNREG Act, namely the entitlement of 100 days of paid work at the statutory minimum wage to an adult member of every rural household, can be seen as the linchpin that holds all three agency types: the relational, the collective and the individual. The relational agency of the MGNREG Act drives this modus operandi in terms of the resources that include enabling both the institutional infrastructure and the financial requirements. The collective agency here acts to facilitate accessing this resource structure; it is the elected assembly in conjunction with the district-level state structures that oversee the work selections, approvals and payments. The work selection process entails coalescing individual demands into a commonly agreed pool of work categories. A certain proportion of the individual agency thus becomes part of the collective agency platform.

As indicated earlier in the section on the achievements of the MGNREG Act, most notable progress was made in the first few years following the implementation of the Act. These included women's workforce participation, income security to the poorest through secured 100 days of work and asset/infrastructure expansion at the village level. These successful outcomes can be easily explained through the interaction of a strong relational agency driving the individual and the collective agencies. This congruence resulted in a healthy uptake of the MGNREGA-related work with regular payments and confidence in the collective platform for grievance redressal. However, more can be learnt regarding the possibilities of the CF to enable the desired outcomes by analysing the fault lines and the pitfalls of the MGNREGA discussed under the section on 'The Pitfalls'.

One of the key fault lines attributed to the weak actualization of the MGNREG Act were found to be in the various dimensions of the village assemblies that were considered central to the successful roll-out of the Act. These, as noted earlier, are the collective agency of the communities through participation in common goals and through their commonly elected representatives. The fault lines in the collective agency are understood better through the four genres of power, as discussed in detail in Chapter 3. The collective agency platform uses the power *with*, that is, power through finding common ground and building collective strength, and a positive disbursement of the power *over*, that is, by bestowing the decision-making authority on the elected office bearers who are lawful members of the village assembly. The privileged members of the village assemblies, in most cases, transformed the positive disbursement of the power *over* to the traditional expressions of power through domination and coercion to benefit the village elite. This in turn appears to have weakened the members' confidence in the collective strength as well as the individual member's willingness either in participating in the village assembly meetings or faith in the grievance redressal system. The outcome has been near collapse of the social audit process, which was much acclaimed for its innovative methods for widening participation of the marginalized and poorest communities in rural India.

At the same time, the relational agency comprising a number of central and state government institutions stumbled in a multitude of commitments and deliverables. These ranged from timely release of funds to creation of a functioning institutional infrastructure required for the MGNREGA activities at the village and the district level accompanied by feeble mechanisms to remedy the failures. The overall consequence was a weakened and ineffective relational agency that had spurred MGNREGA activities and galvanized the individual and collective agency at the village level in the initial years of the implementation of the MGNREG Act. As the Act is relational-agency driven, a weak relational agency in turn loses its capacity to invigorate the individual and the collective agency platform, thus resulting in poor participation in the village assembly, feeble engagement in the MGNREGA activities and loss of confidence in the state institutions.

Convergence framework at the macro landscape

Macro-level development projects such as Fome Zero and the MGNREGA discussed in this chapter are government-initiated projects driven by a strong political will, implemented to address a specific macro-level problem. The projects are resourced and supported by a large institutional infrastructure to facilitate its implementation, that is, a strong relational agency. In such macro landscapes, top-down conceptions, which are an important component of the relational agency, entail engendering an active individual and collective agency platform. It does so by delivering on actions that address the needs and priorities of the people, thus winning their trust. A mechanism to include the voices of the grassroots ensures capturing the problems identified by the people and in shaping the subsequent interventions. This in turn spurs their participation and engagement with the project activities both at the individual and at the collective levels.

In both macro initiatives, three key components that defined the successes of the projects can be identified. These include, *first* and foremost, a strong political will that creates a robust infrastructure of opportunities and support for the most deprived – a well-founded effective relational agency. *Second*, pathways integral to the project to inform and empower individuals and communities. These nurture individual and collective agencies and offer a platform to exercise them. *Third*, strengthening local capacities to implement, monitor and work in close collaboration with the grassroots within a dynamic mechanism that updates the ground realities in real time. This ensures a strong congruence in the three agencies reflecting an opportunity structure that addresses the deprivations experienced by individuals and the communities. Further, an effective relational agency has inbuilt corrective mechanisms to monitor and restore resource leakages, control clientelism and ensure grassroots representation in local decision making.

The formation of the model noted earlier can also be explained using the power discourse lens. The power *over* exercised by both the agents of relational agency and the collective agency is deployed to ensure the institutional infrastructure functions as required and enthuse people into engaging with the project activities, thus espousing active collective and individual agencies in the impoverished communities in the case of Fome Zero and in the villages in the case of MGNREGA. The role of relational agency in such macro-level projects is therefore central to achieving the desired outcomes. As noted earlier, the relational agency itself, though, is reliant on the collective and individual agencies it helps to foster. Therefore, interventions at macro landscapes, which are more often than not relational-agency driven also require functioning individual and collective agencies for any desired transformation.

In both Fome Zero and the MGNREGA, where projects demonstrated functioning relational, collective and individual agencies and a strong congruence of the three, positive outcomes were achieved.

Chapter 5

THE MICRO LANDSCAPE

UNDERSTANDING DEVELOPMENT PROGRESS AT MICRO LEVEL WITHIN THE CONVERGENCE FRAMEWORK

This chapter presents analyses of third-sector and community projects at the micro landscape in different parts of the world within the CF developed in Chapter 3. The selected case studies range from projects in Brazil, UK (London), Uganda and India. The discussions then capture selected micro actors considered as champions of change because of their actions that resulted in positive outcomes for the wider community.

Introduction

The CF developed in Chapter 3 offers a conceptual schema of the conditions needed for achieving the desired outcomes. Shaped by ground research along with observational and interpretive data of a case study in rural Bihar in India, the schema puts forward the CH: *a development intervention is more likely to work when there is congruence between individual goals, collective goals and the relational context*. The relational context here refers to the social-, economic- and political-policy structures. This chapter examines four case studies at the micro level in different country contexts of Brazil, UK, Uganda and India. Analysis of individual drivers follows the case study discussion. Data for much of this chapter is drawn from the author's fieldwork research in these countries as well as long conversations with key individuals in these organizations. The selection of these case studies was influenced by both the tangible shifts in the outcomes of interventions directed towards specific hardships in the community and how the community engaged in the process to address the problem.

The chapter is organized into five sections. Following this brief introduction, the next section investigates the selected case studies with a particular focus on the outcomes and the process of achieving the outcomes. This analysis is situated within the CF to examine the extent or not to which the progress in each case study can be explained by the CH. The third section captures the research conducted by the author with individuals in different contexts, each attributed with driving the change. These individuals sit on a wide spectrum from senior policymaker, project managers, CEO of NGO, NGO workers, grassroots women to subsistence farmer. The fourth section brings together the key argumentations from the previous two sections to highlight the dynamics of progress demonstrated in the selected case studies. The discussions are then followed by the conclusions of this chapter.

The exemplars

Narratives of attainments of desired change or how problems have been addressed in communities are captured in this section. The geographical location of the four case studies spans from Brazil (Instituto Fazendo História in São Paolo), UK (ATD Fourth World in London), Uganda (Mothers Union) to India (Childreach International). An important point to note here is that no claim is made regarding the exclusivity of the selected case studies in terms of what makes them exemplars. There are hundreds of such organizations engaging and driving positive shifts at the micro level all around the world. The examples investigated in this chapter merely illustrate the author's research and discovery from the wide spectrum scattered around the globe.

Instituto Fazendo História, Brazil

Over the last three decades, there has been a conceptual shift in the Brazilian law regarding the rights of children and adolescents. The new legislature introduced in 1990 (the Statute of Child and Adolescent) and further elaborated in 2009 (New Adoption Law) recognizes all children and teenagers as individuals with rights, to be respected as individuals who participate in decisions that affect their lives (IFH, 2015). Within this framework, it is the legal obligation of the family, the society and the state to protect children and teenagers and create an environment where they can achieve their full potential. When families are unable to ensure 'with absolute priority, the effectiveness of the rights to life, to health, to feeding, to education, to sport, to leisure, to vocational education, to culture, to dignity, to respect, to liberty and to family and community relations' (Art 4,Federative Republic of Brazil, 1990), the shelter network is one of the mechanisms guaranteed by the state to protect and safeguard the well-being of these children and teenagers. The shelters embrace these children and teenagers on a temporary basis in the hope that a stable, caring and permanent environment can be found in due course. These solutions can be through improvement in their family circumstances, and they return to their families, through legal adoption, or they are placed with substitute families (foster families).

As per the Brazilian National Survey of Children and Adolescents in institutional care (Ministry of Social Care, 2011), Brazil had 2,624 shelters with almost 37,000 youngsters in care. The five main reasons that push children and teenagers into care are noted (IFH, 2015) to be: negligence by family (37.6 per cent), drug or alcohol addition of parents (20.1 per cent), abandoned by family (19 per cent), domestic violence (10.8 per cent) and homelessness (10.1 per cent). Other causes include poverty, sexual and psychological abuse, mental illness of parents, parents' imprisonment, orphans and parents' illness. This causal matrix for institutional care indicates the fragile and fractured family contexts with the resulting emotional vulnerabilities of the children and teenagers who come to the shelters. The people working in the shelters are therefore required to be skilled, highly driven and devoted to their work beyond the call of duty in the nine-to-five job.

Instituto Fazendo História (IFH) was established in 2005 as a registered Brazilian nonprofit organization. IFH has since then continued to support children in care through a variety of projects, including negotiating long-term godparent relationships between volunteers and children who are unlikely to return to their families or be adopted, and support groups and services for older children to transition them to independent adulthood. The *Fazendo Minha História* (translated as 'Creating My Story', FMH), though, was its central project.

FMH was developed by a group of trained psychologists working in shelters in São Paulo in 2002. These experts realized that many children who were living in the shelter institutions had no records or pictures of their family life. They found that the frequent disruptions in the children's lives, combined with lack of any documented memories, affected children's personal development. The absence of any records on family history also resulted in the shelter care workers having little or no knowledge of the children's past, making it difficult for them to provide the appropriate support for each child. The FMH project was developed to use art and storytelling to help children living in homes and shelters to overcome trauma. FMH's starting point was children's reading practice, using books and literature to promote an enjoyment of reading and of stories about the human experience. Adults, including care workers, volunteers and family members, then talk to children about their stories in a sensitive way. As a result, children would learn to express and value their personal stories. The aim of the project was to cultivate language and expression as tools that every child and adolescent in the shelter can use to own their past and present their story. In addition, this would also facilitate an emotional interaction between the volunteers on the project, the shelter workers and the children.

Over the years, the creation of a scrapbook (called an *álbum* by those involved in the project) has become the centre piece of the approach. Children are supported by designated volunteers, usually with a one-year agreement, to develop scrapbooks documenting key moments in their lives. Volunteers working with smaller children, even infants, may develop scrapbooks with birth records and baby photos; volunteers working with older children walk the children through the process of choosing the content that they want to put in their own albums. This approach has been rolled out well beyond the project itself. IFH godparents also develop albums with their godchildren. Shelter workers and members of the judicial care system have also been trained in the FMH approach and are encouraged to help children document their stories.

The roles of the various actors within the FMH project are clearly defined. The children and the adolescent living in the shelters are the central focus of the FMH approach. Their participation is considered essential for the implementation of the FMH project. The IFH professionals with expertise in this domain provide the training to the shelter workers and the volunteers. The IFH further takes up the project management responsibilities to facilitate its implementation at the shelters. The shelters are expected to adopt the FMH approach of working with the life stories of the children and adolescents living at the shelter. The aim is to embed this in all the educational projects running at the shelter. The educators are important links in the project as they regularly deal with the children, the teenagers and their families. The volunteers too have a crucial role in project. These are individuals who are highly driven and committed individuals who, as per IFH reports, should be 'aware of the motivations which led them to participate in the programme'. This awareness is expected to enable the volunteers to carve out professional relationships and focus on building bonds with the shelter children that do not end abruptly, thus preventing further rupture in the child or the teenager's life. The volunteers therefore need to be willing as well as highly skilled in supporting the emotional needs of the shelter children and adolescents.

The FMH project has multiple stakeholders comprising the children, the adolescents and their families; the shelter professionals; the volunteers and the IFH-trained resource persons deputed on the FMH project. Further, as most shelters are state supported, the social policymakers who can insist or make it mandatory for the shelters to adopt the FMH project are also key stakeholders in the project. The involvement of the social policy makers has been pivotal in the recognition of the FMH methodology within the national policy documents in recent years. This was corroborated during interviews with senior legal experts and policymakers in the country's Ministry for Social Care. These high-level state personnel exhibited detailed insights on the FMH methodology along with the understandings of its potential in the restorative process of the lives of children and adolescents who come to the shelters. The research further revealed the in-depth awareness of the challenges entailed in its implementation and how these might be mitigated to some extent. There was a strong undercurrent of support for making FMH methodology mandatory in all state shelters in the country. This demonstrates the groundwork and effort the IFH would have put into engaging with the policymakers and forging a partnership with key decision makers.

The IFH professionals as well as many of the shelter workers are trained psychologists and educators. The Freirean pedagogical insights are robustly embraced not just in shaping the FMH methodology but also in the partnerships created with the different stakeholders. The FMH principle of helping the child/teenager develop a language and an expression that would enable them to own their past and present with confidence draws on Freire's postulate that through word power each individual can win back the right to say his or her own word, to name the world (Freire, 1970).

Further, bringing in each actor as an active stakeholder who has a specific role along with learning through interaction with other stakeholders and specific learning outcomes is also situated in the Freirean discourse. Here, a key axiom is that *people educate each other through the mediation of the world* (Freire, 1970). The FMH actors become Freire's 'people' and the interaction of these agents through the scrapbook project allows inter- and intra-stakeholder learning. Thus, the child or the teenager is the subject who interacts in cooperation and direct or indirect dialogue with other stakeholders – the shelter workers, volunteers, IFH experts, family members and the state. This results in his or her becoming the author of his or her landscape of memory. Concurrently, the subject develops transformative skills of cognition and skills to communicate their emotion in words. This facilitates being understood by shelter workers and volunteers who can help the healing process. The learning of the other stakeholders includes skills that go beyond theory building on theoretical foundation complemented with praxis. These are critical skills required in the understanding and nurturing of youngsters for a better life. The state officials in particular directly gain insight into how implementation of policy affects social outcomes for children in shelter.

The CF can be shown to resonate somewhat with certain aspects of the Freirean approach. The individual in both constructs is considered an active subject in the world he or she lives in – the individual agency in CF. However, the individual subjects, not just by themselves but by *meeting* each other and through dialogical action, focus their attention to transforming a common challenge they face (Freire, 1970, p. 149). Within CF this process is captured first by the congruence of certain individual agencies into collective agency and second by the congruence of this collective agency with certain relational agency as illustrated in the model in Chapter 3.

Applying the CF to the IFH story of spread and adoption of the FMH methodology by several shelters as well as mention in the National Social Policy documents, some nuances are worth noting. Unlike previous case studies, the state is not strictly part of the relational agency but more an actor in the social care of children and adolescents through supporting the shelter network. The Ministry of Social Care, though, does influence the buy-in of the FMH methodology by the individual shelters. Further, the ministry has raised the profile of IFH by using it as a good practice example in its national policy documentation. These steps have resulted in the uptake of the FMH methodology in several shelters indicated by the area A in Figure 2. This process entails a desire and willingness of each actor in the domain to improve the well-being and life opportunities of the shelter children and adolescents as the central focus. The area A in Figure 2 therefore demonstrates convergence of the multiple stakeholders towards a common goal. The shelters where this convergence had taken place exhibited a friendly and relaxed environment with children that appeared to be well bonded with the staff. They showed genuine excitement and pride in presenting their life albums – 'the scrap books' to the research team. In some shelters, while the staff were keen and enthusiastic about sharing their work on the 'scrap book' project with the teenagers, there was evidence

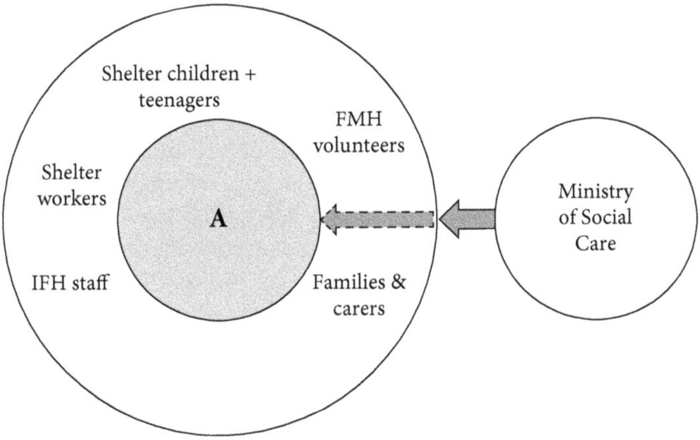

Figure 2 CF and IFH.

of a weak buy-in from the teenagers. This was confirmed by a story of a teenager who had run away several times and was on the run at the time of the research team's visit to the shelter in April 2017.

ATD Fourth World in London, UK

In 1957 while working as the chaplain to 250 families in the emergency housing camp in Noisy-le-Grand, near Paris, Joseph Wresinski founded an organization that became the International Movement ATD Fourth World, with ATD standing for '*All Together in Dignity*'. Wresinski's own experiences of growing up in a poor family, his interactions with the Noisy-le-Grand families and the volunteers he worked with helped formulate his thinking on poverty as violation of human rights. He sought to address this by focusing on the respect and dignity of those in poverty instead through handouts and charity. Wresinski grounded this within a secular context, thus embracing disenfranchised people from all cultures, faiths and races. Drawing on his own early life of multiple deprivations, he was convinced that overcoming poverty required building on what the poor have, resonating with the Well-being Approach to poverty reduction (McGregor, 2006). This included the human capital of people in terms of their intelligence, desire for respect and determination to do something about their situation as well as their strength. Currently, its work spans over five continents with a comprehensive presence in both North and South America, Western Europe, Central and West Africa, the Indian Ocean and East Asia.

The UK ATD Fourth World branch was established in 1968. Currently, its focus is on two main domains: 'Giving Poverty a Voice', which fosters participation of people living in poverty; and 'Together in Dignity', a family support programme that includes advocacy for families in crisis. Projects in the former domain include workshops, training and targeted programmes to inform and upskill those living in poverty to engage with policies that affect their lives. Most of all it provides discussion space for the sharing of experiences and aspirations, planning together and learning from each other. Thus, embedding the strategy within Wresinski's paradigm of valuing each individual to overcome poverty together as a group. The second domain entails supporting the families experiencing multiple challenges by providing a stress-free environment at its Frimhurst Family House. This large Victorian house in Surry can accommodate up to thirty people. With its own expanse of woodlands and greenery, Frimhurst acts as the fulcrum to all the family programmes run by ATD Fourth World UK. It is seen as a safe haven for families to be together, away from the stresses of life they experience, to be able to unwind and think clearly, to share and learn with others in similar situations with dignity and respect for each other. It is at Frimhurst that ATD Fourth World UK enables the community spirit of the families in poverty to flourish. It is also where individuals learn new skills to improve their opportunities in life and overcome poverty as well as to achieve their aspirations.

Some of the multiple challenges that many families face are poor health, inadequate housing and economic insecurities through lack of regular employment, debt and housing arrears. These in turn lead to fear of eviction and the subsequent adverse impact on the overall well-being and resilience. They are then trapped in a vicious cycle that reinforces adversity and inability at each encounter. In many instances, such circumstances result in families being separated by the Social Services as parents are deemed unable to provide a safe environment and care for their own children. The family programmes (FPs) at Frimhurst support and mentor such families harnessing their aspirations, their abilities and strengths as a community. They also work with external agencies involved to help the families overcome their challenges.

Some of the FPs include the 'One-to-One Support', 'Getting Away From It', 'Skill-Sharing' and 'Access to Volunteering'. The central focus of the first two programmes is the empowerment of the family unit. A key inroad into this is through supporting and enabling families to be aware of where and how to seek the correct information so that they can access public services and their entitlements. Very often disenfranchised families are unaware of the support system they can access or lack the confidence to approach the system. Evidence from families who have been part of the one-to-one support indicates that key benefits include confidence building, improved communication within and outside of the family, together with essential skills needed to access information and seek help as the key benefits. Additionally, a unique feature of the project is to consider each family as a unit where all members are affected by a specific issue, albeit in different ways. This is in contrast to many council services and statutory bodies that focus on individuals with a specific problem. The family-centred strategy is in line with the overall objective of helping families to overcome challenges that push them into poverty and being socially excluded. Further, the project offers a safe space for families to reflect on risks, aspirations and goals, thus helping them to identify specific tasks and skills needed to move forward. Recognizing the vulnerabilities and pressures of daily life that poor families undergo, the family-centred approach offers residential breaks at the Frimhurst Family House over the summer and the Christmas to such families.

The 'Giving Poverty a Voice' programme is another noteworthy example of good practice. The programme is conceived to help participants develop their own understanding of the issues that shape their lives; engage meaningfully in the context they live in; and have a say in decisions that affect their lives. This entails empowering the participants through information and knowledge of the current political context, public policy and social service provisions as well as showing them how to access opportunities. Further, it includes expanding the participants' understandings of the specific issues that affect their lives and the importance of engaging with the democratic process. An example of how this was implemented in recent times is illustrated by the series of workshops on human rights and meaning of freedom of expression amidst the BREXIT referendum, followed by presentations by participants at the European Fourth World People's University, Brussels. The focus of this discussion was to demonstrate how multiple deprivations, such as insecure housing, poor literacy and fragile financial positions, can obstruct people from achieving their human rights. Additionally, the project encourages participant engagement in other innovative ways, including museum and exhibition visits to learn and reflect on the history of London and the long existence of pockets of poverty in the city. By considering their own positions within these narratives, the participants not only become more informed about their past and present contexts but acquire the confidence of being someone with a role and value in society.

The ATD Fourth World strategy, evident in all of its projects discussed earlier, demonstrates a sound influence of the Freirian approach that then helps to nurture and shape the individual and the collective agencies of the participants. The ATD Fourth World participant families – the subjects – not just by themselves but by *meeting* other families and through dialogical action focus their attention to transforming a common challenge they face (Freire, 1970, p. 149). Here, a key axiom is that *people educate each other through the mediation of the world* (Freire, 1970, p. 149). The primary premise of the ATD Fourth World ideology, as noted earlier, is to build on the human capital of individuals and families such that they are empowered to pursue their aspirations and goals while enabling the collective spirit of the families to flourish. The empowerment process entails sharing lived experiences of poverty as well as narratives of how they have been able to overcome some of the challenges they faced. This allows the participants – the subjects – to search and reflect on their own positions within these narratives, becoming the Freirian learners. Very often these learners are the disenfranchised families who are unaware of the opportunities they can access or do not have the confidence to approach the system. Sharing the experiences of families who have been part of the ATD Fourth World one-to-one support gain hope and new access to possibilities due to confidence building, improved communication within and outside of the family, together with developing essential skills needed to access information and seek help.

Further, each family unit brings in a unique perspective of the lived experiences of their situation and how they are working to engage in being able to have a say in decisions that affect their lives with a definite role in the society. Thus, the families educate each other through Freire's dialogical process by sharing and exchanging their sphere of information and knowledge. The family units are both learners and educators.

The empowerment of the ATD Fourth World participants shaped by the Freirian dialogical process simultaneously espouses the individual and collective agency of the participants. The participants as individuals and as household units acquire the information and knowledge of the current context, the public policy and social service provisions as well as how to access these opportunities. Thus, they are able to exercise their agencies to engage in activities that will help in addressing the multiple domains of deprivations in their lives. This entails learning new skills to allow them to access opportunities in life and overcome poverty as well as to achieve their aspirations. This also allows them to claim their entitlements and social service support which they could not, due to lack of information and confidence. Figure 3 illustrates this process. Area A represents the population of poor families in the UK while area B represents families that are being supported by ATD Fourth World projects. The ATD Fourth World Freirian influenced empowerment process facilitates the exercise of individual and collective agencies of the family units. This in turn enables them to connect with their social service entitlements, become active citizens and access better new opportunities captured by the relational agency in area C.

Mothers' Union Uganda: The Eagle Project

Mary Sumner established the Mothers' Union (MU) as a society in Alresford, England, in 1876. Driven by her ambition to create an inclusive platform where women from rich, poor and illiterate backgrounds could be part of a network, the aim of the society was to support women to bring up their children in the Christian faith (Mothers' Union, 2016). Within two decades, the society had been registered at the national level bringing together 170,000 members within the umbrella of the belief in marriage, parenting and prayer to be the core foundation of strong families. With Queen Victoria as its patron and following her death, not only did the membership see a sharp rise but its official presence spread to Australia, New Zealand and Canada.

Over the next five decades, the remit and the influence sphere of MU expanded rapidly to include campaigns for raising the minimum age of women to sixteen years, advocacy on issues of marriage and divorce, abortion and religious education and sending delegations to represent these domains in government forums. Additionally, the diamond jubilee of MU facilitated for the first time, funding for development

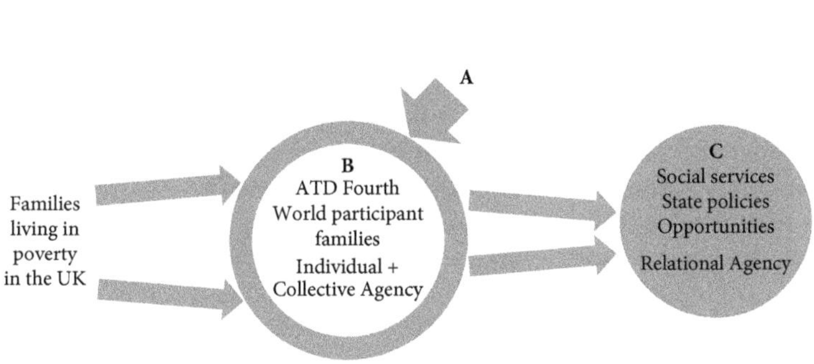

Figure 3 CF and ATD Fourth World.

work in the poorer parts of the world. In the latter part of the twentieth century, the MU underwent further enlargement of its areas of activity and engagement in line with the changing landscape of society. This resulted in the MU's involvement with new issues such as the wider recognition of poverty and its related problems prevalent in the developing world, our moral responsibility to address these issues and also engage with reducing inequality both domestically and globally. Other new domains included ordination of women and homosexuality (Mothers' Union, 2018). While Mary Sumner's conceptualization of prayer and religion as the foundation for strengthening family bonds remains the philosophical underpinning of MU, its work and reach go far beyond the original vision. The MU currently has over 4 million members in eighty-three countries (Mothers' Union, 2018).

In 2012, the MU Uganda launched a pilot for the Eagle Process. The underlying principle of the Eagle Process is to enable the 'church and the community to work together to address common needs by using their own shared resources' (James and Kwarimpa-Atim, 2015, p. 1). The objectives of this approach are to support stable family life, improve relationships, facilitate better livelihoods and promote gender equality. The Eagle Project in Uganda builds on MU's early work in Uganda (Family Life Project) as well as the community mobilization models of the church and the Samaritans. The focus is on helping bring about attitudinal shifts in the communities to embrace care for others and move away from dependency. The project entails three distinct stages – first, church-led workshops to bring shifts in the mindset of the people accompanied with the formation of the community members in Eagle groups. This is followed by implementation of the learning through group and household projects. Second, collective mapping of needs by the community and the church and consensus of priorities. Lastly, taking further the identified problem to be addressed through a project formulation process comprising in-depth research of the issue, planning, delegated community committees leading to implementation and monitoring of the work. The family and community resources are considered core in the design of the project albeit facilitated by external funding as in the case of the Eagle Project in Uganda.[1]

A more detailed analysis of the three stages noted earlier shows that the Eagle Process works through church institutions which are

1. The project received £40,196 from the Isle of Man International Development Committee and £52,105 from MU core funding.

established as safe spaces where community issues can be raised. The next entails creation of linkages between the Eagle groups/initiatives and the government. Through registering Eagle groups as community-based organizations, these community groups are able to access government resources. These resources include sourcing technical training from government officials, for example, from agriculture or health offices, lobbying for material support through local government personnel; provision of seed or support with improving or building roads and bridges. Increased lobbying was also found to have resulted in bringing in health personnel to train on nutrition and primary health and to organize health camps to provide HIV testing and screening for cancer and malaria. Additionally, forging linkages with government schemes and structures also included accessing health camps for vaccinations, testing and screening, school feeding programmes and management committees that ensure better attendance, and drawing on government data for baseline and monitoring purposes.

The process further sought to create linkages between Eagle groups and other NGOs. For example, some dioceses have linked with government-supported projects such as Literacy and Adult Basic Education (LABE), with savings and credit cooperatives, and with other micro-credit schemes such as Pride and Finca. Some NGOs have also contributed to the provision of seed. Connections have been forged between the Eagle groups/initiatives and wider church programmes and expertise. In Madi Nile West, for example, additional training and technical support was provided to Eagle groups through a program called Farming God's Way. Moreover, Mukono linked up with personnel from CMS' 'Samaritan Strategy' to strengthen the new church's envisioning process. The 2016 report (Mothers' Union, 2016) highlights that the Eagle Process has been most effective in the dioceses where leaders at all levels understand how the Eagle Process equips the church to carry out its mission more effectively – rather than just supporting it as an external MU Programme.

The evaluation of the project in 2015 (James and Kwarimpa-Atim, 2015, p. 8) found the largest shift in the domain of agency. This manifested in people taking a lead in addressing their own household or community problems deploying their local resources. These in turn resulted in the overall improvement in livelihood opportunities enabling better access to basic needs. The seven dioceses that adopted the Eagle Project indicated the most tangible change in the realm of initiatives and engagement with problems, followed by improvements in relationships and livelihoods.

However, all dioceses did not show the same levels of attainment (James and Kwarimpa-Atim, 2015, p. 8). Further, much less progress was observed in the dimensions of health and gender equality. This was disappointing as the Eagle Process focused particularly on the inclusion of women in the initiatives. It often manifested into women taking on leadership roles in churches and in the projects. For example, in Madi West Nile, all the Eagle group leaders were women. Increasingly, it is being observed that such processes often result in women taking on the majority of the work. While much research needs to be done to offer evidence-based claims of the increasing demands being placed on women to assist in finding solutions to a plethora of problems ranging from poor sanitation in the community, men's alcoholism in the village to improvement in midday meals, observational research confirms these outcomes. Perhaps extending the UN's HeForShe campaign (UNWomen, 2014) to women's SHGs to include men in the development initiatives as well in tackling community problems along with women.

The successes made in the expansion of initiatives and people owning their problems to search for solutions as well as the three well-defined stages of the project can be analysed within the CF. The latter describes the process by which the former – one of the outcomes of the project – was achieved. The first stage of the process comprises connecting with the community as individuals, albeit in meetings facilitated by MU in the church. The church is perceived as a safe and respected space by the community members where they can raise the problems they experience as individuals, households and community. At this stage, the process initiates a dialogue with individuals who have a strong religious underpinning. This is followed by encouraging the members to engage in a reflexive process that helps them understand their positionality in the wider gamut of their life.

While the Eagle Process does not specifically mention Paulo Freire's work on pedagogy (Freire, 1970), the discourse on conscientization through *problem-posing education* where Freire outlines that when individuals (students in the case of Freire's literature) reflect on the problems they experience with themselves and in the larger world, they develop their ability to gain a critical understanding of the dynamic nature of the real world. Further, they learn to see their position in the changing realities of the world in which they exist. The process leads to a continuum between the problems, existence and action or desire to find solutions. The first stage of the Eagle Process thus resonates with Freire's conscientization and problem-posing methods. The individual community members become aware of not only their complex realities but also possibilities of their engagement to address some of the challenges they face. The process facilitates the individual community members to feel confident and *exercise their individual agencies.*

The second stage of the Eagle Process espouses the Community Eagle groups and the church to jointly map the community needs/problems and agree on priorities. During this phase, then, some of the individual needs and problems common to several members in the community become collective needs and community problems. This is followed by enabling the community to engage with their identified common needs and deprivations collectively, thus transforming individual agency into collective agency demonstrating the *congruence between certain individual agency and collective agency.*

The Eagle Process then carves linkages and collaborations between the Eagle groups/initiatives and the government. This is achieved by registering the Eagle groups as community-based organizations that are then able to access public provisions and government resources. These include technical training in agriculture and health offered by government officials, lobbying for support and investment in the local infrastructure, provision of seed, health camps for screening HIV and other diseases as well as vaccinations. Access to state-supported schemes also includes school feeding programmes and management committees to ensure better attendance and drawing on government data for baseline and monitoring purposes. The partnership pathway adopted by the Eagle Process in this third stage reflects an *overlap with a functioning relational agency.* The relational agency as defined within the CF Model in Chapter 3 indicates the opportunity structure that can be accessed by the poor. The opportunity structure provision in most developing countries is the remit of the governments – albeit more often than not it is weak and inefficient especially in terms of access and delivery. Hence, by forging a relationship with the state, the Eagle groups are able to exercise their collective agency and gain access to the opportunity provision by the state.

In addition to the state-supported opportunity structure, the Eagle Process further creates linkages with other NGOs and with the wider church programmes. As noted earlier, some dioceses have linked with government-supported projects, with savings and credit cooperatives, and with other micro-credit schemes such as Pride and Finca. Some NGOs have also contributed to the provision of seed. Thus, the relational agency within the Eagle Process comprises both state- and non-state-led opportunity provision.

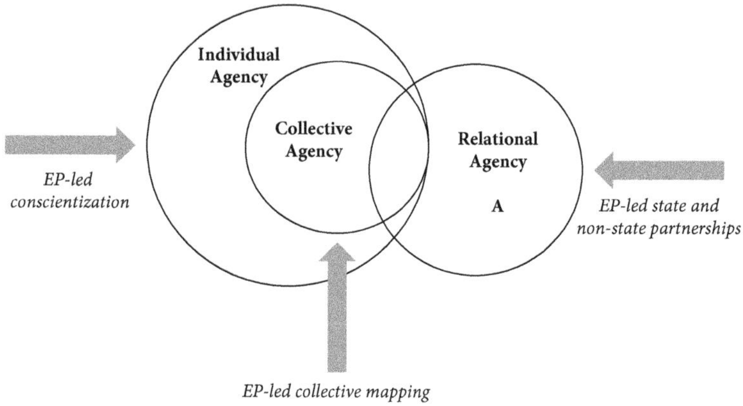

Figure 4 The Eagle Process and CF.

Figure 4 captures the convergence in the three types of agencies and demonstrates how the Eagle Process is enabling the communities to engage and address their problems.

The area A represents progress in engaging the groups to take lead in addressing their own household or community problems by both deploying their local resources and accessing the larger opportunity domain. It also shows the improvement in livelihood opportunities enabling better access to basic need, improvements in relationships and livelihoods.

Save the Girl Child Childreach, Hissar, India

In the early 1990s Amartya Sen put forward the concept of 'Missing Women' based on the low ratio of women to men mostly in China and India. This ratio when compared with sex ratios in developed countries and translated into numbers indicated the number of women who would be alive if the ratio was normal. Sen (1990, 1992) estimated over a million 'missing women'. The last three census data in India shows that the child sex ratio in the country continues to decline from 927 girls born in 2001 to 918 per 1,000 boys born in 2011 (945 girls born to 1,000 boys in 1991). National policy makers and the research community have engaged with the issue and continue to do so through legislation, media and the rich literature on the subject.

The north-western state of Haryana in India has the lowest child sex ratio in the country with 830 girls born to 1,000 boys as per the

2011 census. Responding to the issue of diminishing girl population in the state, the NGO Childreach India (CRI) initiated the project 'Save the Girl Child' in the peri-urban surroundings of Hissar in 2012. The project was fully funded by the corporate Jindal stainless Limited (JSL), which has a significant physical presence in Hissar Town, as part of its CSR. Hissar is one of the more important district towns of Haryana, with rapid industrial growth in steel and cotton industry in the past two decades. Consequently, Hissar recorded highest decadal population growth (48.72 per cent) during this period. Hissar, according to 2011 Census, had a population of 1.7 million and an average literacy rate of 73.20 with a significant gap observed with male literacy being 82.80 and 62.30 amongst female.

The CRI project team's initial groundwork swiftly established that obtaining any direct information on abortion, particularly sex-selective abortion, would not be possible, given the sociocultural context and stringent legislation. Second, the deep-rooted cultural preference for a male child is viewed as support during old age and girls perceived as a liability continues. With increasing access to technology, these perceptions have led to sex-selective abortions - the practice of female foeticide resulting in the skewed child sex ratio. CRI therefore extensively embraced the use of proxies to design its strategies by naming the project 'Girl child and women empowerment' with activities aimed at directly supporting women in multiple domains. These included prenatal support and tracking the pregnancy, as well as skills training for women and girls to improve livelihood opportunities. Further, it adopted a saturation approach with a multi-stakeholder focus that considered all members of the community as stakeholders - adolescent girls and boys, mothers, mothers-in-law, young and elderly men - as well as key community persons - school teacher, health workers, child workers and local medical practitioner.

The activities within this approach included awareness-raising workshops, advocacy, service provision and facilitation. Primary beneficiaries included currently married women (CMW), adolescent girls (Girls Action Groups, GAGs), and in later project cycles boys and men have also been engaged. Local government, educators and health providers are also key participants in a variety of ways, particularly for advocacy and service provision purposes.

An independent evaluation of the project carried out between August and November 2015, concluded that the most tangible impact of CRI's 'Save the Girl Child' project in Hissar has been in facilitating open discussions to bring about awareness, provide information and knowledge in the domains of: how girls are valued in the society; aspirations and rights of girls and women; women's entitlements, women's health and safety concerns. Further, the field data indicated views, societal norms and understandings that reflect an attitudinal shift in accepting the need for girls' education and their potential to make the much-needed contribution towards family income. The preference for boys over girls remains and sometimes explained on grounds of wasted invested in girls' education as they leave home after marriage and cannot provide old age care. Additionally, within the cultural context, it is only the male child that can perform the last rites as well as continue the family name and lineage. While there is considerable evidence to suggest notable progress being made towards the empowerment of girls, indicated by their increased confidence to air their views, attend festivals, participate in school and CRI activities and aspire to have a paid job, girls are still insufficiently valued.

A key strength of the CRI project is the complementarities it has crafted with national-level initiatives as well as relationships with key members of the community. This has been an asset in raising levels of awareness about girls' and women's right to education and the benefits that bring them and to wider society. CRI embraced RTE (Right To Education Act, passed by the GoI in 2009, that guarantees free and compulsory education to children between six and fourteen years old) as a gateway into the full spectrum of issues related to attitudes and position of girls and women in the society. The economic necessities of poorer households together with the realization that educated women can contribute to household incomes as evidenced in the Focus Groups of married women and men is helping to both support girls' education and seek paid employment. The field data further shows that CRI activities have been instrumental towards enabling adolescent girls in particular but the married women as well to articulate their aspirations. This is noteworthy and an important milestone in changing how women value themselves and a female child. The next step would be to facilitate the aspirations into achieved goals.

The application of the CF is useful in understanding how this progress has been achieved by the CRI project in Hissar. CRI's embrace of a multi-stakeholder approach points to collating and capturing the collective agency of different actors. By considering each actor as an active participant with a worthwhile role in contributing to attitudinal and perceptual shifts in how girls are valued in the society, CRI's strategy sits firmly within the Freirean discourse (Freire, 1970). As noted earlier in the analysis of the MU case study, Freire argued that in the 'dialogical theory of action, subjects meet in cooperation in order to transform the world' (Freire, 1970, p. 148). Here the first step is to 'name' the world, implying both the understanding and problematizing of the issue by the stakeholders or the 'subjects', as Freire calls them. The second step within the dialogical theory entails communication amongst these subjects or the stakeholders with varying levels of roles and responsibilities to achieve cooperation towards common goals. This was seen as cooperation to 'transforming the defined world'. Within this process, *people educate each other through the mediation of the world* (Freire, 1970, p. 148) as per a key axiom of the Freirean approach.

CRI's multi-stakeholder construct has engaged with multiple stakeholders with different roles and levels of responsibilities in its efforts to address the falling sex ratio in Hissar. As noted earlier, CRI targeted the root cause of the problem which it identified as the undervaluing of females in the society. The girls and the women are the largest stakeholders with most to gain from the success of the project or most to lose from its failures. CRI's focus on engaging men, boys and key resource persons in the community to help in conceptualizing the issue as a problem of the society and how it affects each household and the community, hence how each member is a stakeholder resonates with the Freirean 'subject' described earlier. A commitment or cooperation to work towards a common goal also demonstrates CRI's efforts towards espousing collective agency in the community. Further, participation of the local law enforcement agency – the state police department, the buy-in from the local state health and education providers as well as CRI's strategy to comprehensively anchor onto the national schemes – indicates reaching out and engaging with the relational agency within the CF developed in Chapter 3.

The area A in Figure 5 shows domains where there has been a strong transformation of individual agency into collective agency and a congruence with the relational agency. This implies that sufficient number of stakeholders have committed to cooperate in working towards CRI activities in addressing the undervalued status of girls and women. Examples of outputs and outcomes include active participation in hands-on information and advocacy workshops followed in due course by allowing girls to join secondary school- and college-level education as well as encouraging daughters-in-law to take up paid work. Other outcomes included, adolescent girls asking to be educated, to be able to go to college, be upskilled and informed of the legal age for marriage. Direct involvement and collaboration of state agencies (police, health providers, child development services) with CRI workshops and

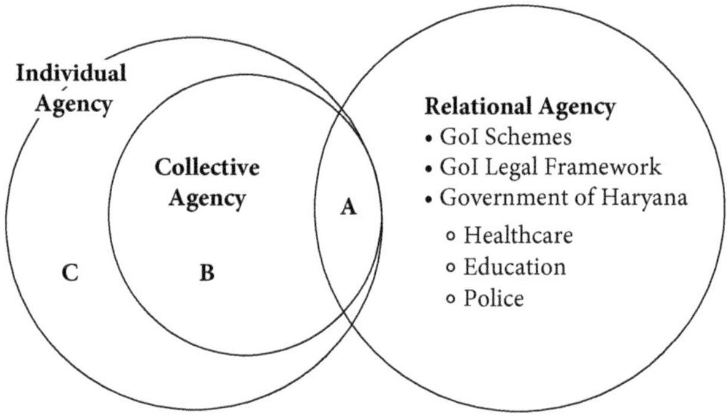

Figure 5 CF and ChildReach International.

activities show convergence in the goals of the state and the community collective agency.

Areas B and C in Figure 5 illustrate the different phases of the CF. The summation of the areas C, B and A represents all the individuals and their respective agencies in the community. Area B indicates the subset of the individual agencies that have coalesced towards one or several common goals. This cohort has come together to act collectively representing the collective agency in the community. It follows then that not all individuals have agreed to be part of this cohort, perhaps because they do not have the same common goal or they are not able to participate in the collective action for personal or societal reasons. This group of individuals is represented by area C.

Area A is the subset of the collective agency area B that engages fully with the healthcare providers, the child development services, becomes aware of the legal framework, their entitlements and is able to access the national schemes. This area captures convergence of individual, collective and the relational agencies in the Hissar community within the larger context of the declining sex ratio by addressing the undervalued status of females in the society. Area A also captures the tangible impacts of CRI's work, such as participation by the community and the state service providers in workshops for awareness, information and knowledge in the domains of: how girls are valued in the society; aspirations and rights of girls and women; women's entitlements, women's health and safety concerns. It also encapsulates the shifts in the societal norms and understandings, albeit at embryonic stages, of the need for girls' education and their potential to make the much-needed contribution towards family income.

The micro unit – champions of change on the ground

David Bornstein (2007), in his book *How to Change the World*, draws attention to the genre of people who solve social problems – the social entrepreneurs as he calls them. Bronstein's social entrepreneurs though are conceived as transformative agents. These are people who take the attributes captured in Schumpeter's (1984) 'creative destruction', Jean-Baptise Say's 'entrepreneur' and Peter Drucker's (1993) 'changing the performance capacity of society' to social sectors. This entails informed and driven citizens such as doctors, lawyers, engineers, social workers, teachers and journalists deploying innovative ideas to tackle barriers to opportunities in the wide spectrum of social domains of education, healthcare and discrimination to name a few. Bornstein refers to these actors as 'restless people' who belong to the citizens' sector.

Bornstein grounds the distinctness of this citizenry through much of the evidence captured in Bill Drayton's organization Ashoka: Innovators for the Public, established in 1978. Drayton started with the desire to find individuals all over the world with new ideas, entrepreneurial ability and ethical underpinning to solve social problems (Bornstein, 2007, p. 11). In less than three decades, just over 1,800 social entrepreneurs had been given direct funding as Ashoka Fellows towards strategy development, forging links with corporates to build social business and acquire credibility through its brand name. Some of the Ashoka Fellows include a school teacher who through her fortitude and drive was able to get the Mumbai City Corporation to adopt her Environmental Studies curriculum, an agronomic engineering graduate in Rio Grande do Sul in Brazil for his efforts to bring low-cost irrigation and electricity to poor households in rural Brazil to bringing micro-credit to poor farmers in Bangladesh.

The importance of individual actors in ushering social change is somewhat dominated by the narrative on the innovative ideas and processes driving the transformation as also noted in Bornstein's work (2007, p. 11). While the Weberian discourse of the 'charismatic leader' (Weber et al., 1968) remains seminal in the social change theory, framing of the individual as the real hero and the power behind social change remains thin. This section highlights invisible individuals with a drive and determination to do something to change their own and their community's circumstances. These individuals would not necessarily fit into Bornstein's social entrepreneur categorization for most of them are not equipped with any novel idea to engender change. Instead, these are people with aspiration and a steely determination latch onto any action and opportunity that offers the potential for improving their own and the community's situation. Such individuals exist in all domains of life and in all parts of the world. The narrative in this section captures some of these micro actors at the grassroots without whose actions, albeit confined to a narrow spatial engagement, would have led to the overall poor uptake of policy initiatives. These actors were interviewed during the author's fieldwork on different projects since 2007. They have been both inspirational and instrumental in shaping the embryonic ideas that resulted in this monograph.

Senior policy maker: Why must a policymaker from the elite and exclusive civil service cadre in India insist on pursuing responsibility for leading rural development and related departments only? There are numerous domains such as urban, industry, education, health that are headed by senior civil servants. This is a story of the development champion who as a policymaker headed the state-supported rural women's SHG network for livelihood promotion – JeeVika. This was a relatively new initiative funded by the World Bank that required an in-depth grasp of the rural problems and intense, hands-on approach to planning, monitoring and evaluation. During several one-to-one meetings as well as feedback from fieldworkers gathered during researching the role of women's collectives in the villages, it was evident that the source of the organizational energy and drive was the CEO – our development champion. The belief in prospects offered to the poorest rural households by the uptake of the project within a context of decades of dismal human development in the state exuded hope and conviction. It did not take long for a critical researcher to fathom that this drive was beyond the attributes of an efficient and dedicated civil servant. It had a sense of ownership, empathy and pride in being given the opportunity to address the problems of chronic social and economic poverties. Other noteworthy visible traits were respect for others and a desire to enable people in their roles to be empowered and flourish, be it the receptionist, the administrative officer, the field programme officer, the community organizers and the facilitators or the rural women as office bearers of the SHGs.

Using the expressions of power discourse put forward by VeneKlasen and Miller (2002, p. 55), our development champion can be seen to be using his 'power over' status acquired through his position of authority and leadership to espouse the other three expressions of power – 'to', 'with' and 'within' – amongst the rural communities as well as amongst the vast number of JeeVika employees in the state. These actions pose an interesting critique of the 'power over' typology, which is associated with a number of negative connotations such as coercion, control, dominance and repression. The exercise of 'power over' to create an environment conducive for collaboration and empowerment of individual and collective agencies demonstrates the potential for positive deployment of 'power over'.

Grassroots SHG woman: The second micro actor is a JeeVika SHG woman married with three young children and schooling up to grade three. The petit emaciated body of the woman living in a thatched mud-walled hut with her family was in stark contrast to the zeal and energy she exuded in talking about how the women's collectives represent hope for addressing the problems in the community. Her grasp of the issues, the detailing in understanding of the processes and aspirations embedded in confidence to strive for a better life stood her well outside of the personality genre expected from her demur physical features. Her clarity in communicating with her peers, with JeeVika resource persons, with researchers and those in authority surpassed the skills of many highly trained people. She told us with pride of her recent selection as the expert resource person to train SHG office bearers in other parts of the state, of her experiences at the various training programmes organized by JeeVika and how she was convinced of the power of the collectives to bring about any social change. This grassroots champion narrated a story of how the SHG office bearers could not get an appointment to see the local policymaker for over a month. She mobilized a larger group of over thirty women to accompany the group to the policymakers' office, resulting in an appointment with the senior officer within hours. She was cognizant of her lack of education as the impediment to being employed as the community mobilizer or hold formal cadre jobs. Her drive, spirit and actions energized several women in the village to join the group and become active participants. After almost a decade of making an acquaintance with her, she was leading the anti-alcoholism campaign in the village in 2017 following the GoB's Prohibition Act of 2014. Despite having received threats, she was determined to carry on with the campaign activities. She had first-hand experienced the decline in domestic violence and the drain on household income together with a better family environment. Her insight into how this could be a model for the male child in particular to not consume excessive alcohol was noteworthy.

While our grassroots champion did not have any 'power over' status, she has exercised 'power to' that helped her to muster the courage and confidence in the belief that she can do something to improve her family's situation and address the problems in the community. This in turn helped her to use the SHG space and platform to seek the support of other members for joint action and realize the potential of 'power with'. This was evidenced by her frequent references to the collective strength of the group being more effective than just herself or a single SHG woman. She exhibited a strong sense of 'power within' from the very beginning by having hope and imagining a better future for her family and the community. Despite her own insecurities and multiple deprivations, she chose to deploy her strengths through 'power within' and 'power to' to achieve 'power with' in the community. The success of JeeVika rests on many similar rural women of its million-plus SHG network.

Sidama, Ethiopian highlands farmer: The southern region of Ethiopia is known as Sidama. It covers an area of almost 7,000 square kilometres with a population density of 506 persons per square kilometre in contrast to the national average of 83 persons per square kilometre. The region has three ecological zones ranging from 500 metres to 3,000 metres above sea level. The highlands in the region, located over the altitude of 2,000 metres, cover a quarter of the Sidama landmass. The mostly agrarian region with a dominance of small farmer holdings is representative of the Ethiopian national landscape. Over the years, the region has experienced increasing food insecurity through a combination of population pressures resulting in dwindling landholding size, erratic rainfall and declining soil fertility (Kebede and Adane, 2011). The main highland crops are enset and coffee while livestock rearing is a key source of income.

Amidst shrinking agricultural productivity with price and climate volatilities, there have been several state-supported agricultural extension programmes to help the farmers. The champion farmer, who was known as the 'model farmer' in the region, was one of the participants of these training programmes. He earned the 'model farmer' title because he was the sole participant from a group of several impoverished farmers who implemented the advice on new and multiple farming techniques. The objective was to reduce dependency on mono-cropping systems and improve soil fertility with better productivity.

The champion farmer's large round thatched hut was home to his six children, wife, four goats and two cows. We caught up with him around midday when he was carrying out repairs to the thatched roof. His children and wife were at school where she was enrolled on the adult learning classes. He was one of the twelve children of his parents. He was told by his father to leave school after grade seven to work on the family farm as he was not destined to be the 'king', and therefore there was no point in further schooling. The champion farmer was determined to give better educational opportunities to his children and had plans to support them to go for higher education. His conviction in the potential of education as an assurance for a better life was so strong that he had encouraged his wife to join the adult learning classes. His pride in showing us the new pit latrine he had constructed for the family was notable. Casually tidying the cover on the well, he explained the importance of keeping the water source covered and walked us around the small landholding. There were apple trees growing in the plot with beans, tomatoes and other local greens. Enset was the dominant plant and remained the staple food for the family, but he had understood the relevance of complementing it with other nutrients. He was experimenting with other grains and spices as per the information and techniques he had learnt at the extension workshops.

The champion farmer's hope and drive could be traced back to his childhood of poor opportunities and belief that he can do something to change his family situation. He searched and accessed all opportunities, albeit small at times, to address the challenges his family was experiencing. While, at the time of this research, he was not part of a village collective or group to promote these techniques, word of his successful experiments had spread in the region and amongst the policymakers. He was swiftly recognized by the officials as the 'model farmer', and they provided further information and support to upskill him and expand his experiments. Additionally, he was being invited to agricultural extension programmes as an exemplar and resource person to encourage and inspire others. The champion farmer's actions indicate the trust in 'power to' by harnessing his potential to shape his aspirations for a better life while acting on his 'power within' by imagining a better life, to begin with and having the hope to achieve it.

Sao Paolo shelter head: During the course of the research in São Paolo in 2017, we met several heads of the institutional care homes for children – the shelters where the IFH was supporting the 'My Story' project. While all came across as inspirational and devoted to the cause of children's plight and fragile well-being, the champion in this narrative stood out. Her distinctness was grounded in her exceptional drive, ownership of every action, effort and outcome regarding children's care that took place in the shelter. The detailing in delivery of each plan and service from children's meals, participatory organization of the living area, activities and social space to dining and kitchen area indicated a hands-on inclusive leadership style. She was herself stylishly dressed, with a charming appearance exuberating confidence and a gentle smile that assured she could be approached by all children and staff. Not only did she have Paolo Freire's quotations and books in her office, but she explained with an impressive insight how useful the approach is for the shelter children's education and overall development as human beings. The meeting with the staff was lively and meaningfully participatory, indicating respect for colleagues within a constructive hierarchy.

Our champion shelter head did have a 'power over' status, albeit a different genre than the champion bureaucrat discussed earlier. She, too, deployed this to engender enthusiasm amongst the shelter staff to give it their best. She further directed it towards 'power to' the individual staff in-charge of specific domains. This was evident in how the kitchen in-charge talked about the organization of the food in terms of the menu being catered to children's taste while keeping in mind the nutritional balance and healthy ingredients, the importance of presentation and cleanliness in the kitchen for making meal-times fun and something to look forward to. A similar positive level of ownership and pride was demonstrated by the colleague in-charge of the facilities. The walls were decorated in consultation with the teenagers. Each room had a selection of comics, storybooks and magazines that reflected the popular trends amongst the teens in the country. These features contributed to the distinctness of the shelter, yet again reinforcing the potential of 'power over' typology in the discourse on change. As in the example of the senior bureaucrat champion discussed earlier, 'power over', which is commonly associated with negative traits, can be a constructive force in ushering change if the individual who possesses it so wishes.

Without such individuals, neither would individual aspiration coalesce into community aspiration, thus harnessing the collective strength of the community, nor would any development intervention or policy be embraced and owned by the community.

Conclusion

Narratives of micro-landscape success examined through four third-sector organizations in different parts of the world, each within the CF, draw attention to some distinct common features. These include the presence of a relational agency that indicates state provision of public policy and social support infrastructure. The strength of how well it functioned and reached out to the marginalized communities varied at both intra- and inter-country levels. In some instances, the third sector complements the feeble state provision of the social infrastructure, as seen in the case of the Mothers Union Eagle Project in Uganda.

Second, the micro-landscape actors galvanized the individual and the collective agencies of its participants using different approaches. Paulo Freire's discourse on conscientization through *problem-posing education* is extensively deployed to empower and invigorate individual and collective agencies in all of the organizations researched within the narratives of micro landscape that have achieved positive outcomes. Albeit not all exemplars discussed in this chapter specify its use and name it in framing their strategy unlike the IFH in São Paulo, the IFH clearly articulates the influence of Freire's approach in the conception and implementation of its flagship project *Fazendo Minha História* ('Creating My Story'). The embrace of the power discourse is also observed but mostly in the form of 'power with' and 'power to' as collective and individual agency.

Third, micro-landscape actors require collaborative partnerships with their constituent grassroots as well as with the public policy and social infrastructure provision to achieve their goals. The micro-landscape actors therefore do not exercise 'power over', focusing instead on forging relationships with the state sector (the relational agency) to facilitate its constituents to access the social provisions and their entitlements. At the same time, these actors put in strategies working to empower the individuals and communities to exercise their agencies to connect with the relational agency.

In addition to the organizational entities that comprise the micro landscape, there are individual micro actors at the grassroots in all domains of life who are the invaluable catalysts in progressing the development interventions and achieving the desired outcomes. These individuals are not Bronstein's social entrepreneurs or the informed and driven citizens such as doctors, lawyers, engineers, social workers, teachers and journalists who deploy innovative ideas to overcome barriers to accessing opportunities in life. They are also not the Weberian 'charismatic leader' (Weber et al., 1968). The champion individuals in this chapter are invisible individuals with a drive and determination to do something to change their own and their community's circumstances within their narrow remit of work. The actions of such individuals make them exemplars of deploying the power discourse to harness individual and collective agencies of the community to achieve the overall improvement in their circumstances.

Investigating the progress made by the four micro-landscape actors and the individual grassroots champions demonstrates the critical role of individual, collective and relational agencies. In domains where the congruence in all three agencies is strong, implying buy-in into the intervention from the individuals, the community and the existence of a functioning public service provision, the outcomes were tangible and embraced by the people with a sense of ownership.

Chapter 6

THE FRAGILE CONTEXT

CAN THE CONVERGENCE FRAMEWORK BE USED TO EXPLAIN HOW SOME DEVELOPMENT WORKS IN FRAGILE CONTEXTS?

This chapter examines how some development works in fragile contexts. Using Lebanon as the case study, the discussions investigate NGOs working in Lebanon to assess if the progress can be explained by the CF.

Introduction

This chapter deploys the CF, developed in Chapter 3, to examine whether some genre of the convergence theory can explain why and how some interventions work in fragile contexts. Lebanon is selected as the fragile context examined in this chapter. This selection is grounded in the author's field research in Lebanon during 2016.

The thematic inquiry of this monograph research investigates why some development interventions have worked. In some instances, creating pathways out of poverty for the most deprived communities, or addressing complex problems to mitigate their impact and in other instances offering resolutions to difficult situations. The study attempts to draw attention to success stories and what made them successful. Within multidimensional understandings of poverty, the inquiry aims to offer insights into causal, enabling and impeding factors for this progress at both macro and micro levels. A theoretical construct that captures this dynamic is deployed as an analytical framework to investigate development successes at both macro and micro levels in several countries located across Latin America, Africa and Asia. In this chapter the construct is applied in fragile contexts to investigate how might things work in volatile and unstable political landscapes. This entails situations of internal conflicts and poor or non-existent capacity of the state to deliver public services to its citizens. While such 'working' interventions and services are likely to be a minuscule proportion of what is needed, these are often of critical nature becoming the lifeline of its users.

The chapter is organized into five sections. Following the brief introduction in section one, understandings of what fragile contexts are and what features qualify countries to be placed in the FS category are discussed in the next section. Lebanon is selected as the fragile context in this study. The third section first offers a brief overview and context analysis of success stories from post-conflict economic recovery in selected countries. It then highlights Lebanon's precarious political trajectory and insecure social terrains that are home to a wide range of socio-economic groupings. The fourth section investigates scattered progress in some domains in the post-war Lebanon examining if this can be explained by the CF. The conclusions of the chapter highlight what genre of the convergence theory can explain why and how some interventions work in fragile contexts.

Fragile context: Why treat it differently?

In 2009 Paul Collier brought to attention the unprecedented geographical shifts in the global poverty terrains. These indicated that the majority of the developing world population was living in countries that were rapidly catching up with the OECD economies (Collier, 2009). Collier's focus wasn't the poorest people living in these countries unlike Sumner (2012) who showed that the majority of the world's poor, up to a billion people, were living in middle-income countries. Collier instead urged the global community to notice the remaining minority of countries that he described as 'fragile states'. The terminology was not new. It was used during the 1990s to describe countries with extreme poverty, political uncertainties, internal volatilities and civil wars. Additionally, drawing attention to the feeble or no institutional capacity of the state for public goods provision, Osaghae (2007) uses 'fragile states' to denote all states with insufficient and insecure capacity. Further, Osaghae spells out features, some or all of which are prevalent in FS. These include poor governance, unstable institutions with weak capacity, exclusionary rule, political violence for change of power or its continuity, civil wars, internal conflict and large displacements of population, endemic corruption and overall low or regressive human development progress. The umbrella label was swiftly adopted within the donor and researcher community, with Somalia, Haiti, Sudan, Chad, Ivory Coast and Liberia representing the first cluster of FS in early 1990s, as noted in Nay (2013).

However, Call (2008) suggests disaggregated and more nuanced use of the terminology as each context poses different challenges that require specific solutions. His different categories include 'collapsed state', 'weak state', 'war-torn state' and authoritarian state.

Collier's meta-analysis of the literature, acknowledging the loose definition of FS, distinguishes between state failure and state ineffectiveness towards the well-being of its citizenry. Albeit, both are captured under the 'FS' label. Starting with the premise that the 'core role of the state is to provide the public goods of security and justice in return for taxation' (Collier, 2009, p. 2), when these objectives are not met by the state, it can be called a failing state. This can happen in the following two ways. First, the infighting of power factions and unpredictable political terrain results in the absence of any form of state, as in the case of Somalia in the early 1990s. This renders any form of state capacity to be feeble and provision of public goods by the state a virtual reality and a theoretical discourse. Within this configuration, coups and rebellions can be frequent occurrences as evidenced in some of the West African states and sub-Saharan Africa in general since 1960. A study by the African Development Bank shows that West Africa experienced over 200 coups between 1960 and 2010, with 45 per cent of these being successful in changing the political power structure (Barka and Ncube, 2012). This implied change of the head of the state and, more often than not, the annulment of any existing constitutional framework. More than half of these took place in the two decades before the end of the Cold War in 1989. Hence, while there is somewhat of a declining trend between 1990 and 2010, political instability remains tenaciously imbedded in the region with sixty-seven coups during this period and the majority located in West Africa.

The literature using a range of theoretical insights to explain factors that lead to coups is extensive. It ranges from cultural pluralism, destabilizing impacts of multi-partyism and ethnic dominance (Jackman, 1978), lack of political participation and political pluralism, poor economic growth and employment (Johnson, Slater and McGowan, 1984), internal factors of greed, power and military spending, problematic colonial heritage (Luckham, 2001) to natural resource abundance led political insecurities. The purpose of this section, though, is to highlight the key features of the volatile context which leads to coups or, as in some countries, the end result of the coups, that is, an unstable or a FS and not examine the coup itself.

The second category of FS is captured through countries with a dominant political elite with a forceful state machinery that works for the continuation of its power with feeble concerns for the masses. Examples of this category of FS can be seen in Zimbabwe and Rwanda during the genocide in 1994. Rwanda was found to have a well-organized functioning state structure that was unfortunately directed towards the mass murder of the Tutsi population in the country, as noted by Collier (2009). The state machinery in Zimbabwe, on the other hand, is directed towards keeping secure its autocratic government that has ruled the country since its independence in 1980. The regime has a proven record of illicit practice to crush political opposition, high levels of neglect in all domains of public service provision and distorted benchmarking against economic stagnation to manipulate expectations (2009). While the majority of failing and ineffective states up to the 1990s were autocracies, many of these countries have since embarked a democratic political system, albeit weak and distorted in many cases. The distortions, in particular, appear to either legitimize a coercive incumbent regime by voter intimidation, vote buying and ballot fraud or the voter is presented with candidates that are all likely to be corrupt, not act in the interest of the masses and abuse power. Examples of the former category can be found in the presidential elections of Nigeria in 2007, Kenya in 2007 and Zimbabwe in 2008 (Collier and Vicente, 2008). Further, recent political events and constitutional changes in Turkey and Russia show close similarities with outcomes in the first category. The second group of voter encounters appear to contest the notion that such distortions are likely to be endemic features of infant democracies transitioning from autocracies. This is exemplified by how many citizens viewed the voter options in the US 2016 Presidential elections as well as in the hastily called June 2017 parliamentary elections in the UK. The caveat here being that voters would be hopeful, actively participating in protests and confident of the self-correcting cycle with more able candidates for the next round of elections. This would be far from the expectations of citizenry in the fragile contexts.

In all genres of the FS, the 'failing/failed' and the 'ineffective' then, there is a political elite. In the first category, though, it is divided into warring factions that seek to gain supremacy over others. The political elite in the second group operates to ensure the continuity of the autocratic state. In both cases the institutional dispensation of public goods provision to the citizens is not the priority of the government. The 'failing/failed' states do not have the institutional capacity while the institutional capacity in the 'ineffective' genre of FS is commandeered for activities including patronage and redistribution of resources towards the political elite to protect the regime (Adam and O'Connell, 1999). Another pervasive feature of such states is the incongruence in the larger goals, objectives and the needs of the political elite and those of the citizens, as noted in Collier (2009) and Besley (2006). Again, keeping the focus to seeking understandings of the FS context rather than the investigation of factors that lead to it, it is not the drivers of incongruence rather how it manifests itself that is of relevance here. For example, deployment of the resource revenue in improving public goods is in the interest of the common citizens while diverting it to state coffers largely towards military spending, patronage activities and redistribution amongst itself are more likely to be the revenue deployment preferences of the political elite. However, it is highly possible and reasonable to have some shared wider goals between the political elites and the citizens. Examples of this may be a clean and disease-free environment. The incongruence arises mostly in how these goals are achieved. Demolition of slums to make way for parks and high-rise buildings to achieve a greener environment is likely to be the preferred way of elites but one that would be rejected outright by the citizens living in the slums. The authoritarian regime may also resort to public goods provision in situations where it might be more effective than patronage in seeking loyalty and support (Collier, 2009).

The literature further examines the role of non-state actors in public goods provision as well as in state-building. Batley and Mcloughlin (2010), acknowledging the contested meanings of the 'fragile-state' label, outline the critical role non-state actors can play in service provision where institutional capacity is feeble and delivery systems are non-existent. Under such circumstances the international agencies often partner with non-state actors such as the communities, NGOs and the private entrepreneurs for immediate relief to the citizens. This direct partnership with the non-state actors for public goods provision can unfold into two different outcomes. First, the possible counterproductive impact on the legitimacy and the sovereignty of the state as noted by Ghani et al. (2005) drawing on early experiences in Afghanistan and through the findings of the DFID's Portfolio Review (DFID, 2009). The former study alerts to the danger of undermining the state if its core functions are delegated to non-state providers. Additionally, service provision by the non-state actors is often dependent on external finance with week sustainability and higher prices. Other negative aspects of non-state providers noted in the DFID Review (2009) include lack of any form of accountability, non-standardization of services and week effort towards local capacity building.

The second outcome of non-state providers in fragile contexts can be considered to sit diametrically to the first set of end results described earlier. While the latter are seen to be impeding state-building, the former are seen as enabling state-building. Using the 'capacity' and 'willingness'[1] categorization of FS, the OECD (2009) promotes a typology-targeted approach to engagement, working with one or both at the same time. This entails supporting non-state actor-led initiatives in situations where the state is broken with arrested development. States that are seen to be transitioning to stability but still with weak capacities to deliver its core functions, the OECD recommends a tripartite arrangement including the non-state actors, the funding agency and the state. Here the state has a stewardship role in policymaking and monitoring while being supported in capacity building.

Hilker (2012) takes the debate beyond generic support and outcomes of non-state providers in fragile contexts to a specific focus on empowerment of communities in such situations. She highlights the distinctness between state fragilities comprising failures in authority, service provision and legitimacy and societal fragilities that include feeble human capital, weak social capital with widespread inequalities and social exclusion. Hilker's framework acknowledges the irrelevance of the 'one-size-fits-all' approach to capacity building in fragile contexts in particular. Instead, a detailed grasp of the FS typology is suggested to then carve a context-specific approach to economic, social and political empowerment of the communities. Empowerment of communities in multiple domains within fragile contexts is considered crucial for upskilling the wider public, reducing social inequalities of education and health, improving livelihood opportunities and offering overall sustainability of interventions through local ownership. These dimensions Hilker notes are comparable to several low-income country scenarios. In a more recent study Jochem, Murtazashvili and Murtazashvili (2016) find that peace building towards strengthening state capacity and democratic institutions in fragile contexts such as that of Afghanistan is highly complex and challenging. However, promotion of democracy at the grassroots is likely to support reconciliation efforts and escalate peace building.

1. Here willingness refers to the direct policy framework accompanied with actions of the state to support human development of the citizens, as described in detail in Brinkerhoff (2007) and DFID (2009).

In summary, the label FS represents a range of state fragility typologies that often have several overlapping features instead of sharp delineations. Drawing on the rich literature exploring the term, these typologies include 'collapsed state', 'weak state', 'war-torn state', 'authoritarian state with arrested development', states with political uncertainties, internal volatilities and civil wars. These can further be located within the state capacity and willingness relationship on

Table 2 Fragile and Non-Fragile State Key Features

Key features	Fragile state (FS)	Non-fragile state developing country (NFS)
Capacity	Feeble or non-existent systems to deliver the core functions of the state provision of public goods low priority, low willingness to achieve pro-poor outcomes	Systems in place to deliver public goods, albeit not always efficient, often in need of upgrade and investment, slow improvements
Institutional infrastructure	High levels of corruption, leakage in public funding, poor accountability, weak institutions that can collapse, geared towards activities that ensure loyalty, patronage, continuity and wealth expansion of the ruling elite	Mechanisms to address injustice and conflict resolution exist, albeit dispensation is weak sometimes, corruption is widespread but not of the same level as in the FS and it is contested openly with official inquiries, mostly judicial independence
Human development	Modest progress but no low-income FS achieved a single MDG (R) Not always the priority of the state	Numerous NFS achieved a number of MDGs though progress needed in many others,
Political regime	High incidence of coups, infighting factions, authoritarian and coercive regimes, highly attenuated political freedoms	Overall respect for the electoral process, intermittent irregularities but mechanism to challenge exists, political freedoms, mostly multiparty structure,
Civil society	Suppressed, fragmented and polarized, weak social capital, low resilience	Vibrant, exhibits strong collective strengths, can be ineffective, occasionally prone to bribery
Examples	Liberia, DR Congo, Zimbabwe	Vietnam, India, Sri Lanka, Brazil

Source: Based on author's research and Brinkerhoff (2007).

the Cartesian plane showing four broad groupings of countries with weak capacity and weak willingness of the state for citizen welfare, weak capacity but strong state willingness, strong capacity but low willingness or low priority for public welfare and strong capacity and strong willingness – the good performers as noted in Brinkerhoff (2007). What stands out in all the typologies of FS is poor public service provision to the citizens, high levels of social and economic poverties amongst the majority population, endemic violence and overall high levels of insecurities. Table 2 captures these FS key features along with what contemporary scenario is likely to be in a non-fragile or stable country context.

The differences identified in Table 2 between FS and the NFS in domains that are essential for development progress in a country robustly suggest that the key actors in the two contexts operate in environments with little similarity. Though, some common grounds, albeit sparse, exist between FS and NFS developing countries. These are not sufficient to fulfil the requirements for the CF, as discussed in this section. The key components of CF are functioning individual, collective and relational agencies. In any of the typologies of FS, these are either far too enfeebled or non-existent. But, some progress has been made in a number of FS (Samman et al., 2018). The next section explores whether the CF can explain what works in fragile contexts.

Does convergence theory explain what works in fragile contexts? Case studies and Lebanon's precarious politics and life amidst volatilities

Hilker (2012) presents a collection of good practice intervention strategies for fragile contexts, while taking cognizant of the invalidity of the 'one-size-fits-all' approach. Her good practice collation is underpinned with a strong context analysis. Examples of success stories include post-conflict economic recovery in Cambodia, Rwanda and Afghanistan; strengthening social and judicial infrastructure through empowerment of individuals and communities in Ethiopia, Afghanistan, Kenya and Cambodia and citizenship rites in Sierra Leonne, Afghanistan, Cambodia and Haiti to name a few. The context analysis in each group indicates strong desire across the citizenry to improve their economic and social situations. These, however, cannot be transformed into the drivers for change due to the restrictions and insecurities experienced by the common people in FS. Neither can these individual desires coalesce into a collective desire that can be directed towards a common or collective action, again due to the restrictions on civil society. This implies weak or non-functioning individual and collective agencies, though the seeds in the form of individual desires that could grow into functioning agency are strong and live in FS. While the functions of the relational agency in the form of opportunity matrix comprising training and mentoring, livelihood openings, subsidies, access to market in the selected good practices examples are facilitated by the UNDP, the case studies indicate full cooperation and partnership of the state. This can be mapped to the stewardship role of the state discussed earlier. External agencies such as the UNDP cannot work in a sovereign state without the full support of the government. The CF under these conditions would then look like as shown in Figure 6.

A further in-depth insight into how the CF can explain what works in FS is offered through detailed examination of the country case study of Lebanon. Lebanon's fragility stems from its religious pluralism comprising eighteen officially recognized confessions with Shiite and Sunni Muslims, Orthodox Christians, Druze and Maronites as key players in the power arena of the country since its independence in 1943 (Höckel, 2007). In recognition of this pluralism fraught with high potential for sectarian conflict to claim power, the constitution was grounded in a system with rigid allocation of political positions and parliamentary seats to each religious denomination. The identity is thus underpinned first with a religious foundation than a national one. Significant change in the demographic landscape since the birth of the country led to the Muslim denominations challenging the Christian denomination on ground of inadequate representation in the power

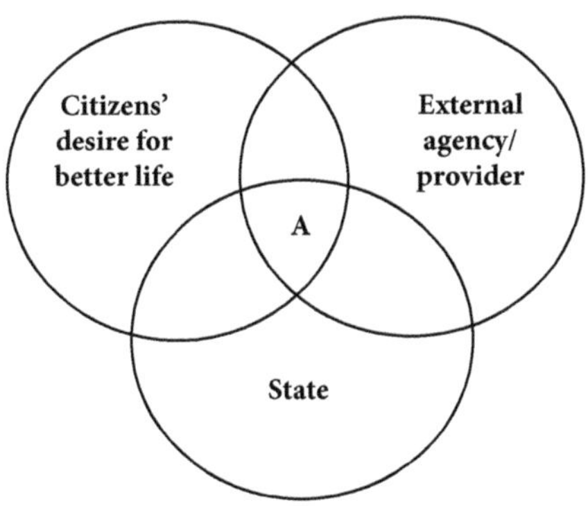

Figure 6 Convergence framework in fragile states.

structure (Höckel, 2007). Despite the confessional affiliation being an integral and a crucial pillar of the constitution, its implementation has been problematic and the root cause of the Lebanese Civil War. The country was left with a fractured society in complete ruins further divided into religious silos in the absence of a unifying national government.

The post-war reconstruction that followed in the early 1990s was even more complex than the pre-war political terrain. Starting with marginalized and a very weak state institutional infrastructure, the process entailed inclusion of the militia warlords into the new political fraternity. While strategically this was successful and important for peace building and reconciliation, it came at the cost of stunting any hopes for the emergence of a democratic system by reinforcing patronage between the citizens and their respective sectarian leaders. The non-functioning state structure allowed the entry of a private entrepreneur to shape the reconstruction and later take up the premiership position of the country. Rafik Hariri's peace and state rebuilding strategy is criticized for its Beirut-centric focus, with the key goal of restoration of economic growth and prosperity in the country. Driven by profit, the plans catered to elites both domestic and those with international links and foreign investors. The wider average citizenry was pushed out of the centre into the urban peripheries, which were in turn ignored by the government and remained without any investment in infrastructure. Thus, the very poor already living in the outskirts and other interior regions of the country did not feature in the direct rebuilding plans. It was assumed that the prosperity and growth in Beirut would eventually trickle down.

The vacuum created by the state in public service provision ushered non-state actors, in particular Hezbollah, thus further adding to the charged nature of the political landscape. The initial disinterest of the government to Hezbollah's entry into the reconstruction of the poorer suburbs of Beirut and the interiors of the country, later reinforced and strengthened Hezbollah's position as a primary player in the political arena (Höckel, 2007). Emboldened in their status in Lebanon and with further support from Iran and Syria, a full war broke between the Israeli Defence Forces and Hezbollah in the summer of 2006 (Accord, 2012). The thirty-four days' war fought on Lebanese soil inflicted close to 1,200 deaths, over 4,000 injured and displaced a little over 2.5 million people. Additionally, it destroyed the investor confidence and the gains made in the tourist industry.

Convergence framework in post-war Lebanon

The post-war rebuilding in Lebanon largely restored Beirut as the financial and business hub and installed a functioning infrastructure in central Beirut. Lack of investment in public service provision in the suburbs and the rest of the country, though, left large sections of the population comprising the average Lebanese citizens and the very poor citizens untouched by reconstruction. This aggravated an already fragmented society widening the divide between the rich and the poor. Das and Davidson (2011), based on a UNDP study of 2008, suggest just over 28 per cent of the population living below the poverty line, with 8 per cent living in extreme poverty. They, however, alert the reader to these figures not capturing the large refugee populations and the foreign migrant workers. This population cohort accounts for some 450,000 Palestinian refugees, 50,000 Iraqi refugees and 200,000 migrant domestic workers. Living with high levels of multiple deprivations in refugee camps, majority of the youth have pledged support to Hezbollah for the only agency to provide for their needs. Höckel (2007) further points to the reinforcement of sectarian divisions through distribution of resources along sectarian lines as part of the appeasement strategy. Examining the post-war rebuilding efforts between the early 1990s and 2005 using the CF shows the absence of any significant congruence between the state, the majority citizenry and the non-state actors. Figure 7 shows the investment focus of the state to promote the interests and prospects of the elite and foreign investors illustrated by the area B. The neglect of public provision in the suburbs and much of the country facilitated the entry of the non-state provider with political and territorial ambitions.

The area A in Figure 7 illustrates the convergence between the needs of the wider citizenry in Lebanon and Hezbollah's self-acquired welfare function to these populations. This in turn led to a significant expansion in its support and loyal constituency. The indifference of the state to Hezbollah's stepping into the service provision void in pursuit of a profit-based reconstruction project benefiting the rich is illustrated by the absence of any convergence between the state, the wider citizenry and the non-state actor. A state within state was created with mounting resentments and rivalries between the different factions leading to the violent assassination of Prime Minister Hariri in 2005 and war with Israel in 2006. The post-war reconstruction strategy between 1990 and 2006 did not recognize or engage directly with all stakeholders in the

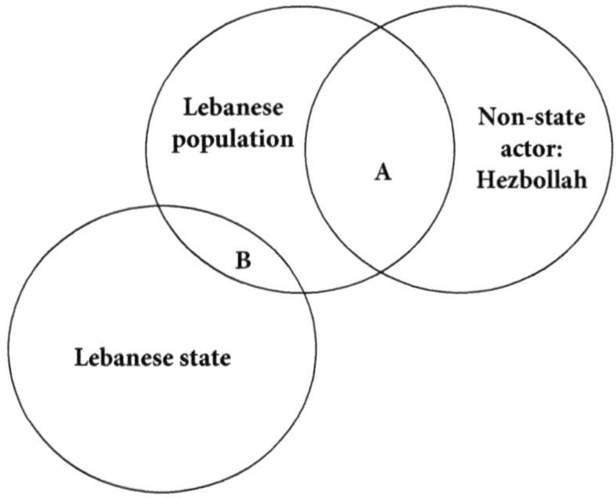

Figure 7 CF in post-war Lebanon (1990–2006).

country. A weakened and fragmented state without any meaingful convergence with the goals of other actors, led to the worsening of the already fractious society and progress that benefited the elite.

The rebuilding of the country since the 2006 war had somewhat a different trajectory than the previous phase. A state institutional infrastructure had emerged which was left with the huge cost of the war of over $1.5 billion, rise in public debt and collapse of the recently restored tourist industry. The damage caused by Israeli air raids and bombings was concentrated in the Shiite impoverished suburbs and the rural interiors. The reconstruction plans therefore had to be drawn with these regions as the epicentre. While Hezbollah was the only influential and active non-state actor with a weak and disinterested state in the pre-2006 reconstruction efforts, the post 2006 efforts included multiple actors, albeit within a highly challenging environment. These comprised a more willing state and better equipped network of state institutions, proactive international donors and agencies, an even more invigorated Hezbollah and a mushrooming network of civil society organizations in the form of new advocacy groups (Accord, 2012). The civil society organizations that had lost their role as complementary agents to the state during much of the twentieth century were once again finding their place in shaping the country. The new advocacy groups were run by volunteers from across the confessional congregations but focused on non-sectarian issues of human rights, women's rights, environment and other public service issues neglected by the state.

It cannot be concluded that Lebanon's new reconstruction strategy steered through the obstacles and achieved notable progress in human development, healing the scars of the prolonged conflict and violent power struggles. What is noted in the literature is that there are far more tangible efforts by all stakeholders to participate in the rebuilding of the country and engage in dialogue to achieve consensus. There are numerous non-state actors including both faith-based organizations and secular organizations without political agendas that have emerged as key providers of public provisions, especially health, education and sanitation. These NGOs are supported by both the state and the international donors. Individuals are able to galvanize local collectives to find innovative solutions to state failures as evidenced by the local NGO for refuge collection in Beirut (Mrad, 2017). The recovery in the post-2006 phase, despite the huge impact of the Syrian war since 2011, is considered more equitable, albeit severe challenges and divisions persist.

Conclusion

This chapter has applied the CF to examine its applicability in fragile contexts. The CF is developed by the author to explain why some development works. The convergence between the three key components, the individual, collective and the relational agencies creates the enabling environment for an intervention to have the desired outcomes for each stakeholder and progress to happen. The literature on FS shows lack of any meaningful collective agency and weak individual agency. Individual desire for better life, though, can be assumed to be omnipresent. The term 'fragile state' is itself a wide umbrella term capturing the feeble or no institutional capacity of the state for public goods provision, all states with insufficient and insecure capacity, states with poor governance, unstable institutions with weak capacity, exclusionary rule, political violence for change of power or its continuity, civil wars, internal conflict and large displacements of population, endemic corruption and overall low or regressive human development progress.

Given the wide variations in the typologies of the FS contexts, the one-size-fits-all approach as in other development projects would be invalid in fragile contexts. Examples of success stories in fragile contexts such as Cambodia, Rwanda, Afghanistan; Ethiopia, Kenya Sierra Leonne and Haiti to name a few show each group with a strong desire across the citizenry to improve their economic and social situations. These, however, cannot be transformed into the drivers for change due to the restrictions and insecurities experienced by the common people in FS. Neither can these individual desires coalesce into a collective desire that can be directed towards a common or collective action, again due to the restrictions on civil society. This implies weak or non-functioning individual and collective agencies, though the seeds in the form of individual desires that could grow into functioning agency are strong and live. While the functions of the relational agency in the form of opportunity matrix, comprising training and mentoring, livelihood openings, subsidies, access to market in the selected good practices examples, are facilitated by the UNDP, the case studies indicate full cooperation and partnership of the state.

Applying the CF in the context of Lebanon further shows that post-war recovery within a CF – albeit in very rudimentary and precarious form – is more equitable, inclusive and focused on the human development of wider citizenry than the non-convergence format of the first phase of reconstruction between 1990 and 2006.

Chapter 7

CONCLUSION

This chapter draws key findings from each chapter and examines the pathways to development within the CF.

The global economic, social and political landscapes have undergone unprecedented shifts in the last two decades. The strides made in social and economic domains, though, are increasingly eclipsed by changes in the geopolitical terrain over the last five years or so. The socio-economic progress includes, amongst others, increase in life expectancy of the world to just over seventy years, improvements in girls' primary schooling with 60 per cent completions, decrease in deaths from natural disasters in the last 100 years to less than half, over 80 per cent of the world's under one-year-olds are vaccinated against some of the killer diseases, over 80 per cent of the global population has access to electricity in some form and the number people living in extreme poverty almost halved (Rosling, Rosling and Ronnlund, 2018). The surge in human longevity in both the rich and the poor countries alike is specifically impressive. A child having survived the first year in Britain was expected to live forty-seven years in 1845 can now expect to live to eighty-one years in 2011. While life expectancy went up by ten years for an average Kenyan between 2003 and 2013, a ten-year Ethiopian child can expect to live up to sixty-one years compared to forty-four years in 1950, as noted by Pinker (2018).

The current discourse is dominated by global challenges posed through political polarization gone too far. Perhaps beyond the tipping point for polarization needed for healthy democracies where dissent, opposition and diversity in thought are considered essential for democracies to function effectively. Carothers and O'Donohue (2019) draw out distinctions between the typologies of political polarization on a continuum with severe polarization on one extremity. Building on the works of McCoy and Somer (2018), the continuum comprises the concept of differential divergence in competing political forces in ideologies and actions to a structured binary division in political life. The latter situation is referred to as severe political polarization where increasingly political thought and policy coalesce around 'us' and 'them'. Further, it creates large factions in the wider society comprising both rich and poor that together represent divisive rivalries. These opposing blocks unleash anger, hate and rejection of peaceful co-existence in social and economic spheres. This in turn constricts the space for dialogue, exchange of ideas, respect for pluralism and grassroots participation in matters that affect the lives of the citizenry.

Carothers and O'Donohue (2019) present an in-depth analysis of the recent spread of severe polarization in several countries that were not long ago living with moderate political polarization that strengthens the democratic tapestry. After two decades of democratic stability, Venezuela and Brazil have both embraced severe forms of political polarization with other Latin American countries too showing strong tendencies. In South Asia, India's claim to the world's largest democracy is under real threat, with the roots of the current leadership in Hindu nationalism over India's seventy years old foundations of a secular democratic nation. Similar examples are found in the Middle East, sub-Saharan Africa and Europe. The 2016 referendum in the UK to leave the European Union saw the most divisive politics, unprincipled tactics and stoking of fears and hatred in a deeply divided society. The partisan politics in the United States has permeated into social and policy arenas traditionally considered outside its remit, even drawing consensus. These include the judiciary, international policy interventions and response to natural disasters. Further, the current leadership style has stoked divisions between 'us' – the supporters – and 'them' – those considered the non-supporters. This has resulted in the spread of polarization in the society to levels befitting conceptualizations of severe polarization.

How do severe polarization tendencies affect the individual, collective and the relational terrains that form the basis of the analytical framework for successful narratives of development in this book? This insight is visited following the key conclusions of the analyses in each of the chapters discussed later.

For now, returning to the central thematic inquiry in this book, *something, somewhere did work, though, to make the positive changes noted in the first paragraph happen.*

The essence of this book has been to capture the epistemic foundations and drivers for these positive changes. A theoretical construct of convergence grounded in field data in rural India is developed and applied to analyse and examine these shifts. The CH proposes that *a development intervention is more likely to work when there is congruence between individual goals, collective goals and the relational context.*

The introductory chapter begins with a brief reflection on the central concern of good and evil in different mythological traditions. While a paradigm of balance restoration between the good and the evil has been the main driver in the history of human kind, goodness can also be its own sphere of action and not always counteracting the negative outcomes. This domain of goodness would include actions such as respect for all genders, other living creatures and the planet. Modern human development domain of addressing a gap or a negative outcome, such as improving opportunities for girls' education or mounting humanitarian effort to combat conflict-inflicted suffering, illustrate the first genre of goodness. The proposition under scrutiny here is whether the global balance is weighted more towards the negative outcomes. The negativity thesis, that is, 'the world is getting worse', is contested by Hans Rosling (Rosling, Rosling and Ronnlund, 2018) and Steven Pinker (2018) amongst others. Rosling uses statistical evidence to counter the negativity instinct by drawing attention to positive trends and outcomes while acknowledging the negatives. Rosling's statistical therapy demonstrates the balance in favour of the positive changes. Pinker calls this the 'Optimism Gap' and the negativity bias and suggests insufficient knowledge to be the driver for failures, negative outcomes and evils. Pinker further points to the gains humankind has made in life, in health by the eradication of infectious and killer diseases, wealth, sustainability, reason, science and human rights over the course of history. So, some development has worked in terms of the evidence-based claims made by both Rosling and Pinker. The positive trends noted here, though, must be acknowledged within larger discourse on the good and the bad that shapes the societal trajectory and not magnified out of proportion to downplay the negatives. There remains much work to be done to achieve a healthy and equitable life for the marginalized communities in the global north and the global south.

Chapter 2 offers a review of the literature on the development trajectory beginning with the establishment of the Bretton Woods institutions over seven decades ago to support nation building in the poorer countries. A roller-coaster pattern of successes and failures can be clearly identified.

The highs and lows of the seven decades of the development journey include a start with two decades of industrialization followed by a somewhat feeble and short-lived wealth redistribution and basic needs agenda. The market approach then returned with vengeance, followed by stringent monetary criteria-led development within a neoliberal rubric. The fifth decade in the 1990s ushered in some hope in the development narrative with a bigger attention to human-centred development. It certainly lasted up to 2008 with widespread buoyant debates on the achievement of the MDGs and the OECD member countries pledge to meet the 0.7 per cent ODA commitment. The seventh decade since Bretton Woods has seen the slippage of the relatively benign period development agenda directed at the poorer regions of the world despite the global consensus around the successors of the MDGs – the Sustainable Development Goals.

The domain of addressing hunger remains one of the biggest failures of the global development project to date, with the World Food Programme (WFP, 2016) indicating one in nine (795 million) people on earth who do not have enough food to lead a healthy and active life. The success stories of improving the lives of the poor living in developing countries are located in both macro and micro contexts and include state and non-state actors. While the macro domains mostly fall within the remit of the state, some large third-sector players also engage with interventions at macro level. State-led achievements indicate an active role of the governments in tackling a development domain that is adversely impacting the lives of the poor. Thus, while Cambodia's attainment in the much-improved healthcare access for the poorest was in partnership with the third sector, India's flagship macro experiment of public works programme NREGA guaranteeing 100 days of paid work was fully a state initiative. There are some notable examples of third-sector-led macro interventions such as Oxfam GB's 'just giving cash' in Vietnam and BRAC's TUP programme in Bangladesh.

The micro-domain stories capture the mostly CBAs to development. Driven by individuals and communities, many of these initiatives include sustainable development activities enabling the use of collective strengths, local knowledge, local resource and its conservation for future generations. While there is a plethora of micro-level stories of progress in the betterment of human lives throughout the world, very few are linked with the macro framework of the state or get scaled-up, working in silos instead. This included the invaluable micro experiments comprising sustainable development activities throughout Africa in the post-SAPs period in the 1980s. However, much of these success stories remained masked under the dismal macro development outcomes of the SAPs era, as noted by Veit et al. (1995). A few other actors are also considered important in shaping development progress and positive change. These include Bornstein's micro actors within the emerging citizenship sector (Bornstein, 2007), political leaders and donors.

It is worth highlighting that the review of the 'Story so far . . .' in Chapter 2 draws attention to the critical role of the state in human development. Further, the institutional capacity of the state, partnership between the state and third sector through macro–micro linkages, grassroots engagement, empowerment and ownership together with collective action are some other factors attributed to successful development outcomes. Additionally, while a full-on engagement with power analysis is somewhat thin in international development, Foucauldian conceptions of power as the ability to change behaviour of individuals or to bring about change – positive or negative – are the basis for its emergence in the development arena. Amidst scattered, albeit emerging literature locating the power discourse within the development landscape, its role in both impeding and enabling progress is undisputed.

Another emerging theme shaping development outcomes is recognition of the critical role of micro actors. These are the individuals whose ideas have improved and made a tangible difference in the lives of multitudes of people. Bornstein's social entrepreneurs (2007) exhibit distinct features of transformative force by spotting the societal problems, ideating a solution and through their sheer determination and belief drive the innovation needed to tackle the problem.

The development story so far then alerts us to be cognizant of the 1990s as the decade when the key development domains improved more than in any other time in history. The achievements are significant given the complexity of the ever-increasing global challenges and failures of the development project often dominating news. This itself is a strong rationale to further investigate why some development works and go beyond what the story so far tells us.

The conceptual schema of the conditions that may be needed for achieving the desired outcomes is developed in Chapter 3. This theoretical construct is grounded in the field research carried out in rural Bihar, India, by the author between 2009 and 2019. While studying the women's SHG network JeeVika for livelihoods and development, a specific situation of irregularities in the state-run PDS for kerosene oil supply and how it was restored by the JeeVika women triggered this inquiry into why did this intervention work. An in-depth analysis of the situation was captured in terms of the typologies of agency and conceptions of power beyond the Foucauldian construction to dimensions of power by Luke (1974) and Gaventa (2006) amongst others. Additionally, insights from Paulo Freire's (1970) work on conscientization further strengthened understanding of the role of individual actors, that is, the women in this case, in bringing about the change. The Freireian discourse asserts that when individuals reflect on the problems they experience with themselves and in the larger world, they develop their ability to gain a critical understanding of the real world. Further, they also learn to experience their *agency in the changing realities of the world in which they exist.*

The framework demonstrated that a convergence of the individual, the collective and the relational agencies achieved through the exercise of different genres of power and conscientization facilitated the desired outcomes in the villages. These included restoring the PDS allowing access to regular kerosene oil, improvements in teacher absenteeism, quality of the midday meal in schools and livelihood means for the poorest in the village. This congruence is the basis of the CF that in turn shaped the CH.

The CF developed in Chapter 3 is applied to study the progress pathways of two macro-level programmes in Chapter 4. These two state initiatives are much acclaimed for changing the landscape of poverty in the host countries. The projects are selected to first examine the validity of CF in explaining the success of state-led large-scale interventions. Second, to test the previous hypothesis within macro contexts. These programmes include Brazil's *Fome Zero* (Zero Hunger) Programme launched in 2003 that later became *Bolsa Familia* and India's National Rural Employment Guarantee Act (NREGA, 2005), which was renamed as the Mahatma Gandhi National Rural Employment Guarantee Act (MGNREGA) in 2009.

The analyses show that the CF indeed captures the mechanics of how the macro-level flagship projects of Fome Zero or Bolsa Familia and MGNREGA were able to make significant progress. Both projects being state-driven demonstrated a strong functioning relational agency, thus offering the opportunity and resource structure, public policy and institutional infrastructure needed to mitigate the problems of hunger and livelihoods, respectively. Further, the emphasis on mobilization of citizens and their participation at all levels in both projects suggests the importance given to collective agency in the communities. The collective agency in Fome Zero was further strengthened through enabling a wider stakeholder participation including the voluntary and private sector through CSR in both cash and kind. This was innovative in fully harnessing the goodwill and energy of the volunteers through a formal channel in the programme with clearly defined objectives. Thus, soon after its launch, close to 100 non-state organizations had become part of Fome Zero on the basis of their social inclusion initiatives. The collective agency platform within MGNREGA is situated within both the members of village assembly and by the elected office holders of the village assembly. Members participating in village assemblies to discuss the MGNREGA work priorities or the grievance redressal process collectively act as one voice pursuing a common goal. The elected office bearers are given the mandate collectively by the villagers to represent them in all MGNREGA matters that concern the village.

All villagers are lawful members of the village assembly and invited and encouraged to participate in MGNREGA matters, thus creating the space for individual agency in the village. Each adult individual who is a resident of the village with interest in MGNREGA, albeit not all have the same levels of desire, constitutes the single units that represent the individual agency. In the case of Fome Zero, its bedrock belief that each individual has the right to food and that this is a key constituent of all other rights – civil, social, economic, political and cultural – indicates its focus on the individual citizens. Additionally, mobilization of citizens and their participation at all levels was considered essential for the progress of Fome Zero. Thus, there was a strong individual agency that aspired to overcome the various dimensions of social and economic poverties that pose challenges to achieving food security.

The analyses further indicate how each agency domain could be strengthened through the deployment of the power (over) located within the relational context of the state. This in turn could espouse other typologies of power to harness the individual and community energies, participation and aspirations. It was also noted that in regions where each agency domain was functioning with a deep common ground and overlapping policy objectives and individual and collective goals, the progress was far more tangible. Regions where the relational agency exhibited weakness through leakages in funds, poor resource structure or feeble infrastructure experienced challenges in accessing entitlements. This in turn led to mistrust and apathy amongst the citizens, eroding the exercise of individual and collective agencies. Such regions were the poor performers in both the Fome Zero and the MGNREGA macro projects.

Overall, then, the analysis of Fome Zero and MGNREGA within the CF validates the CH. The caveat for state-run macro projects is that relational-agency driven by the political will holds paramount importance for macro projects to progress.

The application of CF at micro level through four case studies and individual champions of change in different contexts is presented in Chapter 5. The case studies located at the micro level in the country contexts of Brazil, UK, Uganda and India are non-state initiatives. These case studies were selected because of tangible outcomes of interventions to address specific hardships in the community as well as how the community engaged in the process.

The relational agency in each of these projects comprised the institutional capacity structure of the organization and the wider public-sector service and policy provision. So, for example, the CRI work in India had its own micro organizational structures to engage with the prevalence of foeticide in Hissar as well the state policy and other rights of the girls and women in the constitution it could link up to stop foeticide. How effectively it could draw on the state provision and craft relationships with the policymakers depended on its own institutional capacity. This resonates with relational agency structures of the other three case studies too.

Another feature common to all four case studies was the conceptual resonance with the Freirean discourse (Freire, 1970). In different ways, in all of the four case studies, each actor is considered an active participant with a worthwhile role in contributing to attitudinal and perceptual shifts as well as in becoming the agent of change. The Freirean *conscientization* was visible in all the case studies, leading to a continuum between the problems, existence and action or desire to find solutions. Thus, within MU Eagle Project, individual community members became aware of not only their complex realities but also possibilities of their engagement to address some of the challenges they face. Similarly, the FMH project in São Paulo deployed the Freirean pedagogical insights in not just shaping its methodology but also in the partnerships created with the different stakeholders. This is illustrated by the FMH principle of helping the child/teenager develop a language and an expression that would enable them to own their past and present with confidence. The CRI strategy, enabling adolescent girls as well as married women to articulate their aspirations, how women value themselves and a female child, is located in 'naming' their world. This implied both the understanding and problematizing of the issue by the stakeholders or the 'subjects' as Freire calls them. ATD Fourth World's 'All Together in Dignity to Overcome Poverty' project focus on participation of the 'subjects', that is, people living in poverty not only as recipients but as agents of transformative change in their situation, demonstrates the Freirean underpinning. Each individual in the project is valued for sharing experiences and aspirations, planning together and learning from each other to overcome poverty together as a group.

In all the case studies, the organizations have been the driver for engaging with individual and community stakeholders, to help in conceptualizing the issue as a problem of the society and how it affects them. This in turn encouraged cooperation to work towards a common goal espousing individual and collective agency in the community. Further, both the strength of the relational agency and its congruence with the individual and collective agencies were dependent on the organization's institutional capacity in two key domains. First, drawing in the state into the relational agency structure by anchoring onto the state policy and provisions for the citizens and crafting relationships with the local state agencies as in the case of CRI and ATD Fourth World. Alternatively, this can also be achieved by engaging with the state policymakers to influence the buy-in of the relevant groups/networks into the project as in the case of the Eagle Project and the FMH. Second, in acting as a catalyst for facilitating the congruence of the individual, collective and relational agencies.

Briefly, the application of the CF in micro landscape, while validating the CH, also draws attention to caveats. The relational agency in such interventions requires much input from the micro agent – the organization by crafting relationships to link up with the state provisions and policy structure. Without this, the relational context remains confined to the capacity of the organization, which is more often than not limited. Second, the organization must develop capacity to drive the conscientization process to enable the exercise of individual and collective agencies which in turn engage with the relational context.

The analysis of the champions of change on the ground in this monograph highlights invisible individuals with a drive and determination to do something to change their own and their community's circumstances. These micro actors are neither Bornstein's (2007) social entrepreneurs nor are they the Weberian 'charismatic leader' (1968). While the actions of these grassroots actors were confined to a narrow spatial engagement, without their sustained actions, the overall uptake of policy initiatives would have been poor or another development failure.

Several common features exist in this eclectic group – the exemplars of change referred to in this book. These include a senior policymaker in India, a grassroots women's SHG member in rural India, a small farmer in the highlands in Ethiopia and the head of a children's shelter in São Paulo. First, each of these individuals aspired for better opportunities, not just for themselves but for others beyond their personal network. The determination to do something was embedded in hope and pride. Second, each of these individuals effectively exercised different forms of power. While the senior policymaker used 'power over' to create an efficient institutional infrastructure needed for the policy implementation for rural livelihoods, he also deployed his position to empower the workers and the rural women through the other three genres – power to, with and within. The shelter head, too, used similar power typologies to create an environment where children flourished with a sense of belonging, and the employees worked with a sense of ownership and pride. The farmer and the rural SHG woman exercised power – with and within – to empower themselves and their communities to achieve their aspirations.

The last chapter of this book examines FS within the CF to explore if the CH has any relevance in such contexts. The literature on FS shows lack of any meaningful collective agency and weak individual agency. Individual desire for better life, though, can be assumed to be omnipresent. The term 'fragile state' is itself a wide umbrella term, capturing the feeble or non-existent institutional capacity of the state for public goods provision. It includes states with poor governance, exclusionary rule, political violence for change of power or its continuity, civil wars, large displacements of population, endemic corruption and regressive human development progress.

Examples of success stories in fragile contexts such as Cambodia, Rwanda, Afghanistan; Ethiopia, Kenya, Sierra Leonne and Haiti, to name a few, show each group with a strong desire across the citizenry to improve their economic and social situations. Limitations of insecurities and lack of opportunities restrict the transformation of these aspirations into change of situations. Neither can these individual desires coalesce into a collective desire that can be directed towards a common or collective action, again due to the restrictions on civil society. Therefore, despite non-functioning individual and collective agencies, the seeds of individual aspirations have the potential to grow into functioning agency. While the functions of the relational agency in the form of opportunity matrix comprising training, livelihood openings, subsidies and access to market, for example, are facilitated by the UNDP, the case studies indicate full cooperation and partnership of the state. This suggests that a strong relational agency driven by an external agent and feeble individual agency can achieve development outcomes, albeit its sustainability can be contested on the grounds of external dependency.

Applying the CF in the context of Lebanon in the post-war rebuilding efforts between the early 1990s and 2005 shows the absence of any significant congruence between the state, the majority citizenry and the non-state actors. Instead, the investment focus of the state to promote elite and foreign investors accompanied with neglect of public provision in much of the country resulted in the entry of Hezbollah as the non-state provider with political and territorial ambitions. Thus, there was convergence between the needs of the wider citizenry in Lebanon and Hezbollah's self-acquired welfare function to these populations. This in turn led to a significant expansion in its support and loyal constituency. The state's pursuit of a profit-based reconstruction project benefiting the rich resulted in the absence of any convergence between the state, the wider citizenry and the non-state actor. A state within state was created with mounting resentments and rivalries between the different factions with violent outcomes. The post-war reconstruction strategy between 1990 and 2006 did not recognize or engage directly with all stakeholders in the country. Without any meaningful convergence, a weakened and fragmented state, the outcome was worsening of the already fractious society and progress that benefited the elite.

The rebuilding of the country since the 2006 war had a somewhat different trajectory than the previous phase. A state institutional infrastructure had emerged, which was left with the huge cost of the war of over $1.5 billion, rise in public debt and collapse of the recently restored tourist industry. The post-2006 efforts included multiple actors, albeit within a highly challenging environment. These comprised a more willing state and better-equipped network of state institutions, proactive international donors and agencies, an even more invigorated Hezbollah and an expanding network of civil society organizations in the form of new advocacy groups (Accord, 2012). It cannot be concluded that Lebanon's new reconstruction strategy steered through the obstacles and achieved notable progress in human development. What is noted in the literature is that there are far more tangible efforts by all stakeholders to participate in the rebuilding of the country and engage in dialogue to achieve consensus.

The application of the CF in different context suggests the CH has relevance in each of these distinct landscapes, albeit with caveats and nuances in its application. How is this then affected by the severe polarization discourse briefly discussed at the start of this concluding chapter? Given that severe polarization restricts the participation of some cohorts and thwarts the space for dialogue, it would weaken individual and collective agencies of these groups. The development outcomes could have similarities with the progress of state-favoured group and neglect of the 'others' or even usher in other actors. This has the potential to reinforce divisive politics and destructive divisions and rivalries.

The politics of polarization therefore requires informed engagement by the wider citizenry to avert the threat it could pose. At the same time, healthy polarization that enriches ideas and values needs to be nurtured in the society to enable strong individual, collective and relational agencies. While much work is needed to achieve an equitable, dignified and flourishing life for all in the world, the global consensus to achieve this through the Sustainable Development Goals is encouraging. It builds on the notable progress made in the several dimensions of human life.

Last but not the least, instead, perhaps most importantly given the current context of the pandemic, the CF furthers the understanding of how some countries have managed the Covid-19 with lesser devastating impacts. Countries in this category include New Zealand, Taiwan, Finland, Iceland, Germany, Singapore, Norway and Denmark amongst a few others. Three key features common in the Covid-19-mitigation strategies of these countries are notable. These include a strong clarity and decisiveness shown by the leadership in communicating to the citizens. This was backed by a strong public health support. These indicate a robust functioning relational agency. This in turn espoused individual and collective agency coalescing into the common goal of halting the spread of the virus, resulting in the compliance and cooperation of the citizens. Countries with a stronger congruence of the relational, collective and the individual agencies have achieved far better outcomes in mitigating Covid-19 and continue to do so as the pandemic changes its course.

BIBLIOGRAPHY

Accord (2012) *Reconciliation, Reform and Resilience: Positive Peace for Lebanon*. London. Available at: http://www.c-r.org/downloads/Accord24_Lebanon_ENG_0.pdf.

Adam, C. and O'Connell, S. (1999) 'Aid, Taxation and Development in Sub-Saharan Africa', *Economics and Politics*, 11(3), pp. 225–54.

Agarwal, A. (2016) 'The MGNREGA Crisis Insights from Jharkhand', *Economic and Political Weekly*, LI(22), pp. 38–43.

Aranha, A. V. (2011) 'Zero Hunger: A Project Turned into a Government Strategy', in J. G. Silva da, M. E. Grossi Del and C. G. Franca de (eds), *The Fome Zero: The Brazilian Experience*, pp. 85–109. Brasillia: FAO and Ministry of Agrarian Development.

Bahuguna, R., Pandey, A. C. and Soodan, V. (2016) 'A Study on Socio Economic Impact of Mgnrega on Beneficiaries in Rudrapryag District of Uttarakhand- India', *International Journal of Management and Applied Science*, 2(10), pp. 44–7.

Ballet, J. and Mahieu, F.-R. (2001) 'Enlarged Entitlement Map and Social Capital Indicators as Capabilities', in *Conference Justice and Poverty: Examining Sen's Capability Approach, 5 June 2001*. Cambridge: Cambridge University.

Bank, W. (2015) 'Bolsa Família: Changing the Lives of Millions in Brazil'. Available at: http://web.worldbank.org/WBSITE/EXTERNAL/NEWS/0,,contentMDK:21447054~pagePK:64257043~piPK:437376~theSitePK:4607,00.html.

Barka, H. B. and Ncube, M. (2012) *Political Fragility in Africa: Are Military Coups d'Etat a Never-Ending Phenomenon?*, African Development Bank. Available at: http://www.afdb.org/fileadmin/uploads/afdb/Documents/Publications/Economic%20Brief%20%20Political%20Fragility%20in%20Africa%20Are%20Military%20Coups%20d%E2%80%99Etat%20a%20Never%20Ending%20Phenomenon.pdf (Accessed: June 2017).

Barnes, T. (2013) *Brazil's Bolsa Família: Welfare Model or Menace?* Available at: http://www.csmonitor.com/World/Americas/2013/1117/Brazil-s-Bolsa-Familia-welfare-model-or-menace (Accessed: January 20 2017).

Batley, R. and Mcloughlin, C. (2010) 'Engagement with Non-State Service Providers in Fragile States: Reconciling State-Building and Service Delivery', *Development Policy Review*, 28(2), pp. 131–54.

Belik, W. (2011) 'Mobilization of Enterprises Around the Fight Against Hunger', in J. G. Silva da, M. E. Grossi Del and C. G. Franca de (eds), *The Fome Zero: The Brazilian Experience*, pp. 111–40. Brasillia: FAO and Ministry of Agrarian Development.

Besley, T. (2006) *Principled Agents?* Oxford: Oxford University Press.

Bornstein, D. (2007) *How to Change the World*. Updated edn. Oxford: Oxford University Press.

Bourne, R. (2008) *Lula of Brazil: The Story So Far*. London; New York: Zed Books.

Breitkreuz, R., Carley-Jane Stanton, C. R., Nurmaiya Brady, N., Pattison-Williams, J., King, E.D., Mishra, C. and Swallow, B. (2017) 'The Mahatma Gandhi National Rural Employment Guarantee Scheme: A Policy Solution to Rural Poverty in India?', *Development Policy Review*, 35(3), pp. 397–417.

Brinkerhoff, D. (2007) *Capacity Development in Fragile States*. Maastricht: European Centre for Development Policy Management (ECDPM). Available at: http://ecdpm.org/wp-content/uploads/2013/11/DP-58D-Capacity-Development-in-Fragile-States-2007.pdf.

CAG (2013) *Report of the Comptroller and Auditor General of India on Performance audit report of the Mahatma Gandhi National Rural Employment Guarantee Scheme*. New Delhi. Available at: https://cag.gov.in/sites/default/files/audit_report_files/Union_Performance_Civil_Ministry_Rural_Development_6_2013.pdf.

Call, C. T. (2008) 'The Fallacy of the "Failed State"', *Third World Quarterly*, 29(8), pp. 1491–507.

Carothers, T. and O'Donohue, A. (2019) *Democracies Divided*. Washington, DC: Brookings Institution Press.

Chang, H.-J. (2001a) *Breaking the Mould: An Institutionalist Political Economy Alternative to the Neoliberal Theory of the Market and the State*. Geneva: UNRISD.

Chang, H.-J. (2001b) *Institutional Development in Developing Countries in Historical Perspective: Lessons from Developed Countries in Earlier Times*. Cambridge: Von Hu\0308gel Institute.

Chang, H.-J. (2002) *Kicking Away the Ladder?: Development Strategy in Historical Perspective*. London: Anthem.

Chang, H.-J. (2003) *Globalization, Economic Development and the Role of the State*. Penang: Third World Network; a London: Zed.

Chang, H.-J. (2008) *Bad Samaritans: The Guilty Secrets of Rich Nations and the Threat to Global Prosperity*. London: Random House Business.

Chang, H.-J. and Rowthorn, B. (1995) *The Role of the State in Economic Change*. Oxford: Clarendon Press; New York: Oxford University Press.

Chaudhuri, S. (1998) 'Debates on Industrialization', in T. Byres (ed.), *The Indian Economy: Major Debates Since Independence*. New Delhi: Oxford University Press.

Chmielewska, D. and Souza, D. (2011) *The Food Security Policy Context in Brazil*. Brasillia: International Policy Centre for Inclusive Growth. Available at: http://www.ipc-undp.org/pub/IPCCountryStudy22.pdf.

Cleaver, F. (2007) 'Understanding Agency in Collective Action', *Journal of Human Development*, 8(2), pp. 222–44.

Collier, P. (2009) *The Political Economy of Fragile States and Implications for European Development Policy*. Available at: http://erd.eui.eu/media/Collier.pdf (Accessed: May 15 2017).

Collier, P. and Vicente, P. (2008) *Votes and Violence: Evidence from a Field Experiment in Nigeria*. CSAE Working Paper. Available at: http://www.pedrovicente.org/violence.pdf (Accessed: June 2017).

Culpeper, R., Berry, A. and Stewart, F., ed. (1997) *Global Development Fifty Years after Bretton Woods*. Basingstoke: Macmillan.

Das, R. and Davidson, J. (2011) *Profiles of Poverty: The Human Face of Poverty in Lebanon*. El Metn-Lebanon: Dar Manhal-Alhayat.

Davies, R. (2012). Blog post on the criteria for assessing the evaluability of a theory of change.

Deaton, A. (2013) *The Great Escape: Health, Wealth, and the Origins of Inequality*. Princeton: Princeton University Press.

DFID (2009) *Engagement in Countries in Fragile Situations: A Portfolio Review*. London: Department for International Development.

Dikshit, G. and Sharma, S. (2017) 'Success of MGNREGA: Delusion or Reality – Study of Tonk District, Rajasthan, India', *International Research Journal of Social Sciences*, 6(4), pp. 18–26.

Dreze, J. 2015. 'India's Rural Jobs Programme: A Dismal Appraisal', 4 May, *Huffington Post*. Available at https://www.huffingtonpost.in/jean-draze/nrega-a-dismal-appraisal_b_7202650.html.

Dreze, J. and Khera, R. (2015) 'Understanding Leakages in the Public Distribution System', *Economic and Political Weekly*, L(7), pp. 39–42.

Drucker, P. F. (1993) *Innovation and Entreprenuership*. New York: Harper Business.

Easterly, W. (2015) *The Tyranny of Experts: Economists, Dictators, and the Forgotten Rights of the Poor*. New York: Basic Books.

Ehmke, E. (2012) 'Ideas in the Indian Welfare Trajectory', *Journal für Entwicklungspolitik*, XXVIII(1), pp. 80–102.

Ehmke, E. (2016) 'India's Mahatma Gandhi National Rural Employment Act: Assessing the Quality of Access and Adequacy of Benefits in MGNREGS Public Works', *International Social Security Review*, 29(2), pp. 3–27.

Elson, D. (1997) 'Economic Paradigms Old and New: The Case of Human Development', in R. Culpeper, A. Berry and F. Stewart (eds), *Global Development Fifty Years after Bretton Woods*. Basingstoke: Macmillan.

FAO (2015) *The State of Food Insecurity in the World*, Food and Agriculture Organization of the United Nations. Available at: http://www.fao.org/3/a-i4646e.pdf.

Federative Republic of Brazil (1990) *The Statute of the Child and Adolescent*. Available at: https://www.refworld.org/pdfid/4c481bcf2.pdf.

Ferreira, F. H. G., Leite, P. G. and Ravallion, M. (2008) 'Poverty Reduction without Economic Growth? Explaining Brazil's Poverty Dynamics, 1985–2004'. Available at: http://documents.worldbank.org/curated/en/169731468226737145/pdf/wps4431.pdf (Accessed January 2017).

Fosu, A., ed. (2013) *Achieving Development Successes*. Oxford: Oxford University Press.

Freire, P. (1970) *Pedagogy of the Oppressed*. London: Penguin Books.

Gaventa, J. (2003) *Power after Lukes: An Overview of Theories of Power since Lukes and their Application to Development*. Available at: https://www.powercube.net/wp-content/uploads/2009/11/power_after_lukes.pdf (Accessed: November 29 2016).

Gaventa, J. (2006) 'Finding the Spaces for Change: A Power Analysis', *IDS Bulletin*, 37(6), pp. 23–33.

Ghani, A., Lockhart, C. and Carnahan, M. (2005) *Closing the Sovereignty Gap: an Approach to State-Building*. Working Paper 253. London. Available at: https://www.odi.org/sites/odi.org.uk/files/odi-assets/publications-opinion-files/2482.pdf (Accessed: June 2017).

GoI (2013) *Twelfth Five Year Plan (2012–2017): Faster, More Inclusive and Sustainable Growth*: Vol. 1. New Delhi. Available at: http://planningcommission.gov.in/plans/planrel/12thplan/pdf/12fyp_vol1.pdf.

GoI (2016) *National Health Mission, Bihar Health Indicators*. Available at: http://nrhm.gov.in/nrhm-in-state/state-wise-information/bihar.html (Accessed: December 2016).

Goñi, E., Humberto López, J. and Servén, L. (2011) 'Fiscal Redistribution and Income Inequality in Latin America', *World Development*, 39(9), pp. 1558–69.

Graziano da Silva, J. C. (2019) *From Fome Zero to Zero Hunger: A Global Perspective*. Rome: FAO. Available at: http://www.fao.org/3/ca5524en/ca5524en.pdf.

Green, D. (2008) *From Poverty to Power: How Active Citizens and Effective States can Change the World*. Oxford: Oxfam.

Green, D. (2012a) 'Theories of Change = Logframes on Steroids? A Discussion with DFID', *From Poverty to Power*. Available at: http://www.oxfamblogs.org/fp2p/?p=10071 2016].

Green, D. (2012b) 'Theories of Change = Logframes on Steroids? A Discussion with DFID', *From Poverty to Power*. Available at: http://www.oxfamblogs.org/fp2p/?p=10071 2016].

Green, D. (2016) *How Change Happens*. Oxford: Oxford University Press.

Hall, A. (2006) 'From Fome Zero to Bolsa Família: Social Policies and Poverty Alleviation under Lula', *Journal of Latin American Studies*, 38, pp. 689–709.

Hanlon, J., Barrientos, A. and Hulme, D. (2010) *Just Give Money to the Poor*. Sterling: Kumarian Press.

Hewitt, T. (2000) 'Half a Century of Development', in T. Allen and A. Thomas (ed.), *Poverty and Development into the 21st Century*, pp. 289–308. Milton Keynes: The Open University.

Hilker, L. (2012) 'Empowerment in Fragile States and Situations of Fragility', in OECD (ed.), *Promoting Pro-Poor Growth: The Role Of Empowerment*. Available at: https://pdfs.semanticscholar.org/20b0/f49bcd187d8b9e0115cdeff7a8cad34b45ca.pdf.

Höckel, K. (2007) *Beyond Beirut: Why Reconstruction in Lebanon did not Contribute to Sate-Making and Stability*. Occasional Paper No. 4. London:

London School of Economics. Available at: http://www.lse.ac.uk/internationalDevelopment/research/crisisStates/download/op/OP4%20Hoeckel.pdf (Accessed: May 10 2017).

Ibrahim, S. (2006) 'From Individual to Collective Capabilities: The Capability Approach as Conceptual Framework for Self-Help', *Journal of Human Development*, 7(3), pp. 397–416.

Ibrahim, S. and Alkire, S. (2007) 'Agency and Empowerment: A Proposal for Internationally Comparable Indicators', *Oxford Development Studies*, 35(4), pp. 379–403.

Ibrahim, S. (2008) 'Collective Agency: Wider Freedoms and New Capabilities through Self-Help', in J. L. Dubois (ed.), *Repenser L'Action Collective: une Approche par les Capabilitiés*. Paris: Réseau IMPACT Network.

IFAD (2019). Available at: https://www.ifad.org/en/web/operations/country/id/india (Accessed: August 2019).

IFH (2015) *Instituto Fazendo História Annuall Activities Report*. Sao Paulo. Available at: https://www.fazendohistoria.org.br/results.

ILO (2014) *World Social Protection Report 2014/15: Building Economic Recovery, Inclusive Development and Social Justice*. Geneva. Available at: http://www.ilo.org/wcmsp5/groups/public/---dgreports/---dcomm/documents/publication/wcms_245201.pdf.

Jackman, R. W. (1978) 'The Predictability of Coups d'Etat: A Model with African Data', *American Political Science Review*, 22(December), pp. 1262–75.

James, C. and Kwarimpa-Atim, D. (2015) *The Eagle Process, The Mothers' Union, Uganda*. The Mothers' Union. Available at: https://refugee.jliflc.com/resources/eagle-process-mothers-union-uganda/.

Jochem, T., Murtazashvili, I. and Murtazashvili, J. (2016) 'Establishing Local Government in Fragile States: Experimental Evidence from Afghanistan', *World Development*, 77, pp. 293–310.

Johnson, T. H., Slater, R. O. and McGowan, P. (1984) 'Explaining African Military Coups d'état, 1960–1982', *American Political Science Review*, 78(3), pp. 622–40.

Kebede, D. and Adane, H. (2011) *Climate Change Adaptations and Induced Farming Livelihoods*. Available at: http://www.utviklingsfondet.no/dcg/assets/documents/Publications/1059-dcg_report_no._64.pdf.

Kenny, C. (2011) *Getting Better*. New York: Basic Books.

Khera, R. and Nayak, N. (2009) 'Women Workers and Perceptions of the National Rural Employment Guarantee Act', *Economic and Political Weekly*, 44(43), pp. 49–57.

Kume, H., Piani, G. and Souza, C. F. (2000) 'Instrumentos de Politica Comercial no Periodo, 1987–1998', mimeo, Instituto de Pesquisa Econômica Aplicada.

Lawson, D. J., Hulme, D., Matin, I. and Moore, K. (2010) *What Works for the Poorest?: Poverty Reduction Programmes for the World's Extreme Poor*. Rugby: Practical Action Publishing.

Lin, N. (2001) *Social Capital: A Theory of Social Structure and Action.* Cambridge: Cambridge University Press.

Lockwood, M. (2005) *The State They're In: An Agenda for International Action on Poverty in Africa.* Warwickshire: ITDG Pub.

Luckham, R. e. a. (2001) *Conflict and Poverty in Sub-Saharan Africa: An Assessment of the Issues and Evidence*, p. 128. Brighton, Sussex: Institute of Development Studies.

Luke, S. (1974) *Power: A Radical View.* London: Mcmillan.

Malhotra, A. (2003) 'Conceptualizing and Measuring Women's Empowerment as a Variable in International Development', in *Measuring Empowerment: Cross-Disciplinary Perspectives*, Washington DC, 4–5 February.

McCoy, J. and Somer, M. (2018) 'Polarization and the Global Crisis of Democracy: Common Patterns, Dynamics and Pernicious Consequences for Democratic Polities', *American Behavioral Scientist*, 62(1), pp. 16–42.

McGregor, J. A. (2006) *Researching Wellbeing: From Concepts to Methodology.* WeD Working Paper 20. Available at: http://www.bath.ac.uk/soc-pol/welldev/research/workingpaperpdf/wed20.pdf (Accessed: August 2018).

Mrad, N. A. (2017) *The 81-Year-Old Woman Inspiring a Nation to Recycle.* BBC. Available at: http://www.bbc.co.uk/news/magazine-40191270 (Accessed: June 8 2017).

Nay, O. (2013) 'Fragile and Failed States: Critical Perspectives on Conceptual Hybrids', *International Political Science Review / Revue internationale de science politique*, 34(3), pp. 326–41.

NSSO (2013) *Key Indicators of Employment and Unemployment in India, NSS 68th Round, July 2011–June 2012.* New Delhi: Government of India.

ODI (2016) *10 Things to know about Progress in International Development.* Overseas Development Institute. Available at: https://www.odi.org/sites/odi.org.uk/files/odi-assets/publications-opinion-files/10217.pdf (Accessed: December, 2016).

OECD (2009) 'Service Delivery in Fragile Situations: Key Concepts, Findings and Lessons', *OECD Journal on Development*, 9(3), pp. 7–60.

OECD (2014) *Social Expenditure Update.* Available at: https://www.oecd.org/els/soc/OECD2014-Social-Expenditure-Update-Nov2014-8pages.pdf (Accessed: January, 2017).

Osaghae, E. E. (2007) 'Fragile States', *Development in Practice*, 17(4/5), pp. 691–9.

Oyen, E., ed. (2002) *Best Practices in Poverty Reduction: An Analytical Framework.* London: CROP International Studies in Poverty Research, ZED Books.

Pereira, A. W. (2015) 'Bolsa Familia and Democracy in Brazil', *Third World Quarterly*, 36(9), pp. 1682–99.

Pinker, S. (2018) *Enlightenment Now: A Manifesto for Science, Reason, Humanism, and Progress.* St Ives: Allen Lane.

Putnam, R. (2000) *Bowling Alone: The Collapse and Revival of American Community.* New York: Simon and Schuster.

Raghavan, M. (1999) 'Targeting India's Public Distribution System', *Economic & Political Weekly*, 34(26), pp. 1682–83.

Rao, N. D. (2012) 'Kerosene Subsidies in India: When Energy Policy Fails as Social Policy'. Available at: https://ssrn.com/abstract=2047018 (Accessed December 2016).

Ravallion, M. (2009) *A Comparative Perspective on Poverty Reduction in Brazil, China and India*. Available at: http://elibrary.worldbank.org/doi/pdf/10.1596/1813-9450-5080.

Rawlings, L. (2004) *A New Approach to Social Assistance: Latin America's Experience with Conditional Cash Transfer Programs*. Washington, DC: World Bank. Available at: https://openknowledge.worldbank.org/bitstream/handle/10986/11 (Accessed: January 28 2017).

Riley, J. C. (2005) 'Estimates of Regional and Global Life Expectancy, 1800–2001', *Population and Development Review*, 3(3), pp. 537–43.

Rodgers, P. J. (2008) 'Using Programme Theory for Complicated and Complex Programmes', *Evaluation*, 14(1), pp. 29–48.

Rosling, H., Rosling, O. a. and Ronnlund, A. a. (2018) *Factfulness*. London: Sceptre.

Rowlands, J. (1997) *Questioning Empowerment: Working with Women in Honduras*. Oxford: Oxfam, GB.

Samman, E., Lucci, P., Hagen-Zanker, J., Bhatkal, T., Simunovic, A. T., Nicolai, S., Stuart, E. and Caron, C. (2018) *Fragility, Crisis and Leaving no One Behind*. London. Available at: https://www.odi.org/sites/odi.org.uk/files/resource-documents/12424.pdf.

Schumpeter, J. A. (1984) *Capitalismo, socialismo e democracia*. Rio de Janeiro: Zahar Editores.

Sen, A.K. (1985b) 'Well-being, Agency and Freedom: The Dewey Lectures 1984', *The Journal of Philosophy*, 82, pp. 169–221.

Sen, A. K. (1990) *More than 100 Million Women Are Missing*. New York: New York Review of Books. Available at: https://www.nybooks.com/articles/1990/12/20/more-than-100-million-women-are-missing/.

Sen, A. K. (1992) 'Missing Women', *British Medical Journal*, 304(6827), pp. 587–8.

Sen, A. (1999) *Development as Freedom*. Oxford: Oxford University Press.

Serageldin, I. and Grootaert, C. (2000) 'Defining Social Capital: An Integrating View', in P. Dasgupta and I. Serageldin (eds), *Social Capital: A Multifaceted Perspective*. Washington, DC: World Bank.

Shah, M., Mann, N. and Pande, V., eds (2012) *MGNREGA Sameeksha: An anthology of research studies on the Mahatma Gandhi National Rural Employment Guarantee Act, 2005, 2006–2012*. New Delhi: Orient Blackswan.

Silva da, J. G., Grossi Del, M. E. and Franca de, C. G. (2011) *The Fome Zero: The Brazilian Experience*. Brasilia: Ministry of Agrarian Development. Available at: http://www.fao.org/docrep/016/i3023e/i3023e.pdf (Accessed: September, 2016).

Stein, D. and Valters, C. (2012) *Understanding Theory of Change in International Development* JSRP Paper 1, JSRP and TAF collaborative project, LSE, London. Available at: http://www.theoryofchange.org/wp-content/uploads/toco_library/pdf/UNDERSTANDINGTHEORYOFChangeSteinValtersPN.pdf (Accessed: November 23 2016).

Sumner, A. (2012) 'Where Do The Poor Live?', *World Development*, 40(5), pp. 865–77.

Svedberg, P. (2012) 'Reforming or Replacing the Public Distribution System with Cash Transfers?', *Economic and Political Weekly*, 47(07), pp. 53–62.

Takagi, M. (2011) in J. G. Silva da, M. E. Grossi Del and C. G. Franca de (eds), *The Fome Zero: The Brazilian Experience*, pp. 53–83. Brasillia: Ministry of Agrarian Development.

Tiwari, M. (2014) 'Capability Approach, Livelihoods and Social Inclusion: Agents of Change in Rural India', in S. Ibrahim and M. Tiwari (eds), *The Capability Approach: From Theory to Practice*, pp. 29–51. Basingstoke: Palgrave Macmillan.

UNESCO (2013) UIS Fact Sheet. UIS Information Paper. Available at: http://uis.unesco.org/sites/default/files/documents/fs26-adult-and-youth-literacy-2013-en_1.pdf (Accessed: November 2016).

UNICEF (2016) *The 2016 State of the World's Children Report*. Available at: http://data.unicef.org/resources/state-worlds-children-2016-statistical-tables/ (Accessed: January 31, 2017).

Union, M. (2016) *Mothers' Union Annual Review*. Available at: ttps://www.mothersunion.org/resources?nid=5565#views-exposed-form-resources-default (Accessed: February 2018).

Union, M. (2018) *Mothers' Union, Christian Care for Families*. Available at: http://www.mothersunion.org/media-centre/our-history (Accessed: February 2018).

UNWomen (2014) *HeForShe Impact 10X10X10*. Available at: http://www.unwomen.org/en/news/stories/2016/9/press-release-heforshe-university-parity-report (Accessed: February 2018).

Veit, P. G., Mascarenhas, A. C. and Ampadu-Agyei, O. (1995) *Lessons from the Ground Up: African Development that Works*. Washington, DC: World Resource Institute.

VeneKlasen, L. and Miller, V. (2002) *A New Weave of Power, People and Politics: The Action Guide for Advocacy and Citizen Participation*. Oklahama City: World Neighbors.

Vogel, I. (2012) *Review of the 'Theory of Change' in International Development*. Available at: https://assets.publishing.service.gov.uk/media/57a08a5ded915d3cfd00071a/DFID_ToC_Review:VogelV7.pdf (Accessed: November, 2016).

Watts, J. (2013) 'Brazil's Bolsa Familia Scheme Marks a Decade of Pioneering Poverty Relief', *The Guardian*. Available at: http://www.theguardian.com/global-development/2013/dec/17/brazil-bolsa-familia-decade-anniversary-poverty-relief (Accessed: 30 January 2017).

Weber, M., Fischoff, E., Roth, G. D. and Wittich, C. (1968) *Economy and Society: An Outline of Interpretive Sociology*. Edited by Guenther Roth and Claus Wittich (Translators: Ephraim Fischoff [and others]). New York: Bedminster Press.

Weisdorf, J. L. (2005) 'From Foraging to Farming: Explaining the Neolithic Revolution', *Journal of Economic Surveys*, 19(4), pp. 561–86.

Weiss, C. H. (1995) 'Nothing as Practical as Good Theory: Exploring Theory-Based Evaluation for Comprehensive Community Initiatives for Children and Families', in J. Connell, A. Kubisch, L. Schorr and C. Weiss (eds), *New Approaches to Evaluating Community Initiatives: Concepts, Methods and Contexts*, pp. 65–92. New York: Aspen Institute.

Wetzel, D. and Econômico, V. (2013) *Bolsa Família: Brazil's Quiet Revolution*. The World Bank. Available at: http://beta.worldbank.org/en/news/opinion/2013/11/04/bolsa-familia-Brazil-quiet-revolution (Accessed: January, 21 2017).

WFP (2016) 'Hunger'. Available at: https://www.wfp.org/hunger/stats (Accessed: December, 2016).

Zmerli, S. and Castillo, J. C. (2015) 'Income Inequality, Distributive Fairness and Political Trust in Latin America', *Social Science Research*, 52, pp. 179–92.

FURTHER READING

Bornstein, D. (2007) *How to Change the World*. Updated edn. Oxford: Oxford University Press.

Bowles, S., Durlauf, S. N. and Hoff, K. (2006) *Poverty Traps* (edt). Princeton: Princeton University Press.

Carothers, T. and O'Donohue, A. (2019) *Democracies Divided*. Washington, DC: Brookings Institution Press.

Criado Perez, C. (2019) *Invisible Women: Data Bias in A World Designed for Men*. London: Chatto and Windus.

Easterly, W. (2015) *The Tyranny of Experts: Economists, Dictators, and the Forgotten Rights of the Poor*. New York: Basic Books.

Frances, S., Gustav, R. and Samman, E. (2018) *Advancing Human Development*. Oxford: Oxford University Press.

Freire, P. (1970) *Pedagogy of the Oppressed*. London: Penguin Books.

Green, D. (2016) *How Change Happens*. Oxford: Oxford University Press.

Hickel, J. (2017) *The Divide: A Brief Guide to Global Inequality and Its Solutions*. London: Cornerstone.

Lawson, D. J., Hulme, D., Matin, I. and Moore, K. (2010) *What Works for the Poorest?: Poverty Reduction Programmes for the World's Extreme Poor*. Rugby: Practical Action Publishing.

Pinker, S. (2018) *Enlightenment Now: A Manifesto for Science, Reason, Humanism, and Progress*. St Ives: Allen Lane.

Pritchett, L., Sen, K. and Werker, E. (2017) *Deals and Development* (edt). Oxford: Oxford University Press.

Raworth, K. (2017) *Doughnut Economics*. London: Penguin Random House.

Rosling, H., Rosling, O. a. and Ronnlund, A. a. (2018) *Factfulness*. London: Sceptre.

Sen, A. (1999) *Development as Freedom*. Oxford: Oxford University Press.

Sen, A. (2005) *The Argumentative Indian*. New York: Allen Lane, Penguin Books.

Shiva, V. (2020) *Reclaiming the Commons: Biodiversity, Indigenous Knowledge and the Rights of Mother Earth*. London: Synergetic Press.

Smillie, I. (2009) *Freedom from Want*. Sterling: Kumarian Press.

Tiwari, M. (2014) 'Capability Approach, Livelihoods and Social Inclusion: Agents of Change in Rural India', in S. Ibrahim and M. Tiwari (eds), *The Capability Approach: From Theory to Practice*, pp. 29–51. Basingstoke: Palgrave Macmillan.

Yunus, M. (2007) *Creating a World Without Poverty*. New York: PublicAffairs.

INDEX

Page numbers followed with "n" refer to footnotes.

www.ingramcontent.com/pod-product-compliance
Ingram Content Group UK Ltd.
Pitfield, Milton Keynes, MK11 3LW, UK
UKHW020207290926
15470UKWH00001B/50

9 781786 993601